MULTIPLY YOUR LIVING SPACE

MULTIPLY YOUR LIVING SPACE

How to Put an Addition on Your Home at a Cost You Can Afford

DAN BROWNE

McGRAW-HILL BOOK COMPANY

New York • St. Louis • San Francisco • Toronto
Düsseldorf • Mexico

ALSO BY DAN BROWNE:
The Housebuilding Book
The Renovation Book

The author acknowledges with thanks the very considerable help
of Kevin McCloskey, who did all the drawings for this book.

1234567890MUBP78321099

Library of Congress Cataloging in Publication Data

Browne, Dan.
Multiply your living space.
Includes index.
1. Dwellings—Remodeling. 2. House construction.
I. Title.
TH4816.B75   690'.8'37   78-9706
ISBN 0-07-008485-8

For East-West House

CONTENTS

4 Preparing the Interior for Finishing

5 Interior Walls

6 Floors

7 Finishing the Electrical Work and Plumbing

Appendix of Building Materials 117

Index 121

MULTIPLY YOUR LIVING SPACE

INTRODUCTION

After building a sumptuous heart-redwood, brick, and glass house in California and helping the owners move in, I returned to upstate New York determined to build an addition to the small cabin on several wooded acres my wife and I own. We'd already agreed on its major features but fortunately, although I did not think so at the time, several feet of snow made starting impractical. We were new to the area and decided to spend time looking over the local building supply situation. I was appalled at the prices, although they were actually slightly lower than what I'd just been paying for identical materials in California. However, out there, as the builder, I had shrugged off inflation as a fact of life and simply elevated my own prices accordingly. Here, I reacted as a homeowner with nowhere to pass on inflated costs. I have built many additions and more than a hundred custom houses, but this was my first time on the receiving end and I decided to do all I could to avoid being a passive victim of exorbitant costs. I realized that this meant departing from my well-worn commercial route of lumber and masonry yards, electrical and plumbing supply houses, and I began looking for alternatives.

In a short while I found a local sawmill and bought all construction lumber at less than half the cost I would have had to pay at a lumber yard. As the snow melted, I rediscovered a huge slab of slate on the site that I had intended to remove with a bulldozer. I began to quarry the slate with a flat bar and 2-pound hammer and within a few days had enough pieces for the exterior walls, several interior walls, and a fireplace. While I was digging a trench for the sewer line, my pickaxe struck a roundish rock and split it. There were brilliant colors inside and I was reminded of split-stone work I had done many years before. Splitstone became one of the bathroom walls. As a commercial builder I had shied away from stone because it was expensive and, more important, not readily available at masonry yards but as a homeowner I relearned the fact that not only was stone abundant and free, but also a superlative building material and the simplest and easiest to work with of all masonry materials.

One day I went to the sawmill to check on my order for construction lumber and found the sawyer cutting a beautiful maple log into boards for fork-lift pallets. I asked how he could use such a fine wood for that purpose and he answered that it made no difference to him what he was cutting and if I wanted maple, I could buy it at the same price as fir or any other wood he handled. That conversation led to a maple-plank floor for the addition and built-in white pine dressers and cabinets. Not only did I get maple at 10 percent its commercial cost, but an excellent flooring material was made available that I could not otherwise afford to use.

As a builder it is impractical for me to use secondhand materials, but as a homeowner I searched for them at wrecking yards and flea markets. I bought gem boxes for 5 cents each (they're 79 cents at electrical supply houses), copper fittings, light fixtures, tile, an old hand-painted china basin with a marble counter and accumulated numerous other items at a fraction of their costs if purchased new.

These and other rewarding experiences along the nontraditional route of obtaining supplies had a cumulative result in an addition far superior to what we'd originally planned at a cost of $11.50 per square foot, less than a third the cost of a standard addition of inferior materials. Recounting the specific ways this was accomplished is one of the prime objectives of this book.

One needs also to know how to transform lumber and all other materials into an addition. I have shown the entire building process in detail to demonstrate how the structure is actually put together. The procedures and techniques presented are based on a lifetime of practical construction experience. I have personally performed every aspect of building many times under the exacting requirements of professional construction. Helping the reader erect the addition in an efficient manner that also results in a well-built structure is another prime objective.

No single book can deal with all possibilities in building an addition, nor can all the working processes be completely detailed. I have limited myself to essentials and highlighted parts of the process an inexperienced homeowner might not be aware of or would have difficulty performing. I have dealt in greater length with electrical, plumbing, framing, masonry, and other phases of construction in earlier books and suggest their use if more information is desired, but all you will really need to build an addition can be found here.

Based on firsthand experience, it is my conviction that inexperienced homeowners are perfectly capable of building an additon. My last experience involved two young men who helped me build the house in California. Neither had any previous experience, yet with no more than the equivalent of the information in this book, they were able to install plumbing, wiring, framing, roofing, and all other work needed to complete the house. (One man has since become a contractor and the other a student chef.)

Building the additon yourself is the best means of using exemplary materials and getting a structure that expresses your tastes and needs at a dramatically lower cost. A less obvious but equally important reward is the strengthening of your own self-reliance, a quality that is fast becoming essential in order to cope with mass-produced junk at ever-increasing prices. If this book provides a tool in fashioning self-reliance, its goal will have been achieved.

Materials prices mentioned in this book were accurate in mid-1978 when this book went to press. Such costs have been rising 12 percent a year and there is little likelihood that they will go down or remain stable. Expect to pay more for every kind of material you buy if you're contemplating an addition in 1979 or later. The important thing to remember, if you're building the addition yourself, is that the ratio *for what you can do yourself as against what you have to hire somebody else to do will remain exactly as described in this book.*

WHAT YOU NEED TO KNOW BEFORE YOU BEGIN

1

Local authorities have mapped and divided almost all populated areas into zones that specify what you may build by way of an additon. The most relevant restrictions are setbacks—the closest you may build to your property lines. Setbacks vary greatly; on one street in a particular zone a minimum of 20 feet may be required between the addition and side property lines while an addition on an adjacent street that happens to lie in another zone will have 5-foot minimums or none at all. As you begin to explore the possibility of building an addition, a visit or phone call to your local building department is essential to find out what zone your house is in and the setbacks required at the front, sides, and rear. You may learn that you can extend your house in any direction for greater distances than you need or that the existing house already occupies the maximum allowable building area and an addition is feasible only by adding another story. These examples are extremes and most often, particularly in heavily populated suburban areas where lots tend to be small, the only allowable place to build an additon is at the rear of the house.

Once the required setbacks have been determined, the dimensions should be marked on the plot plan of your house or the survey which banks require for a mortgage. It will now be apparent where it is feasible to locate the addition and its maximum dimensions.

The next step in the exploration is to decide the size of the addition. For the most part, this will be determined by your intended use, tastes, and budget. Let us say, for example, that the addition is to be a bedroom and bath.

The drawing and dimensions are typical of the majority of additions built each year and I will use it throughout as a working blueprint. The 5-by-8-foot bathroom is the smallest that works well. The fixtures are located against the common wall (shared with the existing house) in order to keep piping to a minimum and also locate them in an interior wall as a protection against freezing. Usable space in the bedroom and closet is above average, and after comparison with similar spaces in your home their dimensions can and should be altered to suit your particular needs.

At this writing, using moderate-priced materials, I would charge $16,800 (or $42 per square foot) to erect this addition. To this figure I would add $2200 for plumbing costs—making a total of $19,000, an amount lower than most builders would charge.

Many homeowners will find $19,000 more than

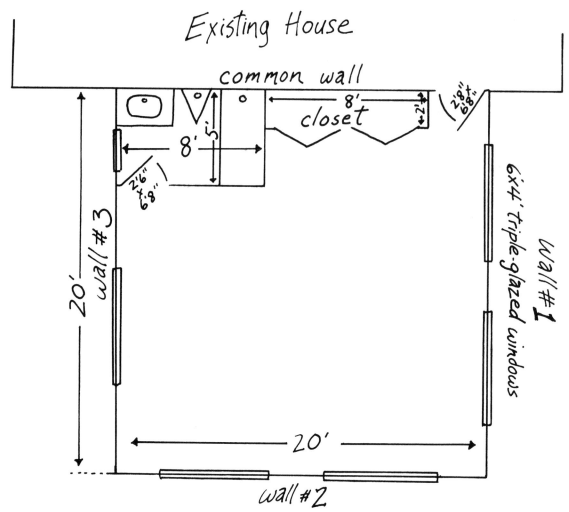

Existing House

common wall

closet

8'

2'8"x 6'8"

wall #3

20'

2'6" 6'8"

8'

5'

6'x4' triple-glazed windows

wall #1

20'

wall #2

Bedroom and bath addition

they can afford and begin to search for means of lowering the cost. One way of doing this that immediately comes to mind is to reduce the size. However, before this choice is made, keep in mind that as the area of an addition is decreased, its cost per square foot rises. A 300-rather than 400-square-foot addition, 25 percent less in area, will not cost 25 percent less. The price will be $46 per square foot or $13,800. Plumbing costs will remain the same, making a total of $16,000 for the smaller addition versus $19,000 for the 25-percent-larger addition. Similarly, a 200-square-foot addition will cost about $50 per square foot and larger-than-average additions as low as $30 per square foot. You will obtain the greatest value if you plan an addition as large as feasible within your budget, although the total cost will be higher. I have yet to meet a homeowner who was sorry to have the

larger addition, but I have returned on several occasions to enlarge additions that proved too small.

The size of the addition (and every other aspect as well) should conform to your tastes; if you like small rooms, by all means plan them this way. However, if you like larger rooms but fear the cost, do not surrender your preference since there are many ways of reducing costs and I will detail the means of accomplishing this throughout. The cumulative effect of many cost-saving items may very well enable you to build an addition large enough to suit you.

Having situated the addition and chosen a size that fits your needs and tastes, you will now want to plan what the structure will look like.

In all likelihood, your house has an outline similar or identical to one of the drawings. The vast majori-

4

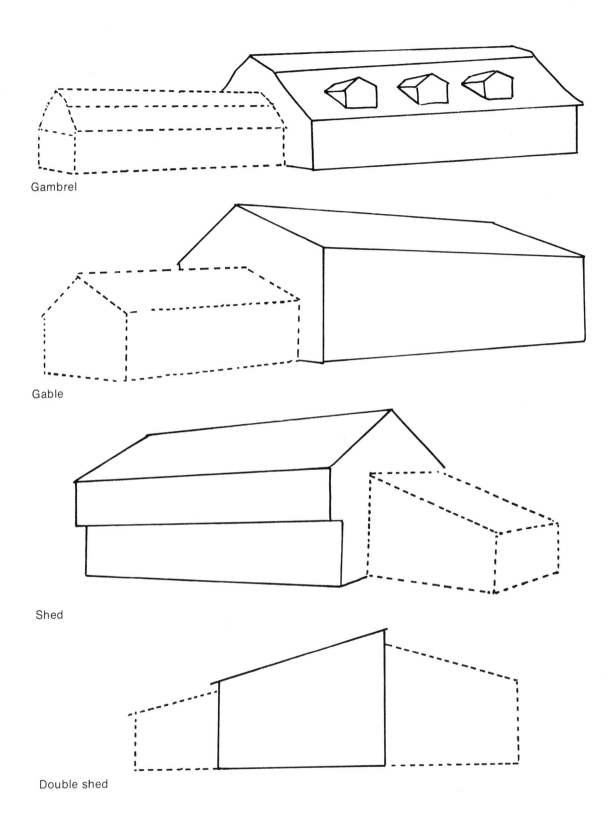

Gambrel

Gable

Shed

Double shed

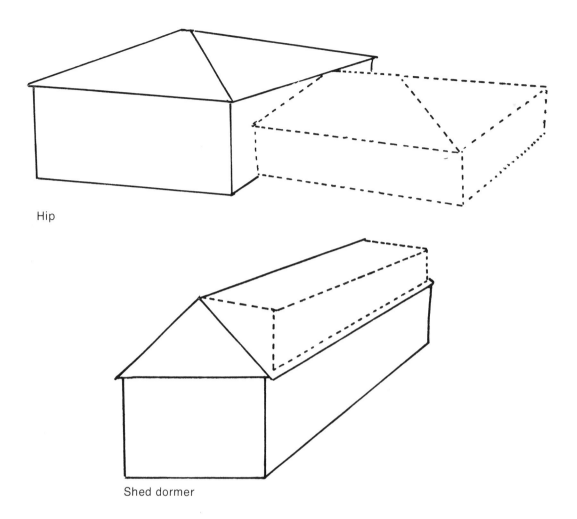

Hip

Shed dormer

ty of homeowners prefer additions in the same style as the existing structure and the additions drawn with dotted lines are those actually built in large numbers. There are variations, and most likely you will see many while driving about that may be useful in visualizing your addition in outline after completion. Most libraries have magazines and books devoted to design that present plans for additions and may also be helpful in showing the exterior shape of the addition and how it relates to the house. If you find a shape you like, working blueprints can be obtained at a nominal cost (usually under $20), from *House and Garden*, Conde Nast Publications, 350 Madison Ave., New York, N.Y. 10017, and similar publications. Homeowners almost always want items such as siding, roofing, windows, and the like to be identical or as similar as possible to items in the house and prefer that the addition appear as if it had always been part of the original structure. This approach eliminates making decisions on materials to use and in many

instances works out well aesthetically and economically, but may have serious drawbacks. For example, if the siding of the house is redwood and one insists on the same for the addition, a particularly high-priced material will have to be purchased. The resulting cost will be excessively high when compared to other materials equally good but substantially cheaper. The soundest approach is to remain flexible about all materials until each has been investigated and specific choices made from a number of options rather than being imposed arbitrarily by the existing structure. There is no need at this point to fill in the outline with details, and doing so may steer you away from your best choices.

I've found that most people who wanted the additon to look exactly like their house had never considered other possibilities. The drawing of the stone silo-shaped addition to a converted barn and the others shown are only a few examples of what can be done with a nontraditional approach. By

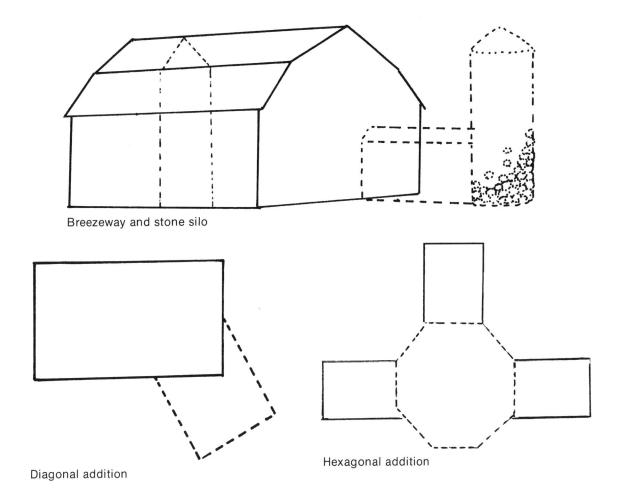

Breezeway and stone silo

Diagonal addition

Hexagonal addition

merely placing the addition on a diagonal at the corner of the house, an unusual appearance is created. Joining three traditionally shaped wings with a hexagonal addition makes an interesting structure. Many ordinary houses have been changed spectacularly for the better by distinctive additions, and this possibility should be considered before a traditional approach is selected. By *distinctive* I do not mean that the addition must be unique, although I am partial to one-of-a-kind-structures. I am speaking of an appropriate addition to your house that is not standard and provides an appearance that best expresses your taste.

Designing a distinctive structure is not an easy job. If you can't come up with a concept at this time, suspend the effort until you have examined all the other aspects of building the addition, since more specific information may be needed. At that time, if you are still unable to design a distinctive addition, consult an architect. This is one of the few situations where I find hiring an architect desirable.

I would also consider hiring an architect if you have very little land on which to build or have special needs such as those of a doctor intending to use the space professionally. Ordinarily, an architect's fee is 10 percent of the cost of a house and more in the case of additions.

At this point, even if you are unable to settle on a shape for the addition and may not do so for some time, you will want to know more about what is involved monetarily since even the least amount may be more than you can afford. A price of $42 per square foot for an average addition presupposes that you will engage a builder to buy all materials and supply all labor. At this rate the materials will be of moderately good quality: redwood, vinyl, or aluminum siding, cedar shingles, panel doors, Andersen windows, oak floors, and similar items. You have a right to expect white pine paneling or its equivalent over the interior walls, proper wiring inside them, and ceramic tile on the bathroom walls and floor. If you begin to substitute cheap materials of good quality, such as asbestos shingles on the exterior and sheetrock over the interior, the cost per square foot will go down significantly. However, there is a limit to lowering the cost without using junk, and it would be unrealistic to expect a figure under $30 per square foot after all economies of this nature are made.

If $30 per square foot is still more than you can afford, building the addition isn't feasible unless you are prepared to reduce the cost even further by taking part or all of the responsibility away from the builder. If, for example, you obtain all materials, it is quite possible to lower your cost to $26 per square foot.

The addition I am building to my house provides a good example of how to do this. I am buying construction lumber from a small local sawmill at $170 per thousand board feet. (A board foot is 1 inch by 12 inches, 1 foot long.) The lumber yard I use as a builder charges me $290 per thousand. For reasons that are irrelevant here, it is impractical for me as a builder to buy directly from a sawmill, but as a homeowner I can afford to use the lumber yard only as a last resort. I have also bought white pine and maple for walls and floors at a cost that is a third and a fifth of lumber-yard prices. In this and similar ways, the cost of the addition is significantly reduced.

If you assume the responsibility of hiring all labor but do not perform any yourself, you should reduce the cost even further—to $24 per square foot—since you will be saving a part of the builder's profit.

If you perform all labor as well as obtain the materials, there is an excellent possibility of bringing the cost down to $18 per square foot.

The figure of $18 per square foot was my original estimate of the cost of building my addition. I envisaged the use of moderate-priced materials and that my wife and I would perform all labor. As I began thinking more as a homeowner and less as a builder, I soon saw how to obtain finer materials than I had intended and still stay within my estimate. As I developed more alternatives to buying from a lumber yard and thus obtaining the greatest value for money spent, I have now revised my estimate and am reasonably sure that my final cost will be under $12 per square foot. A short while ago I would have believed that this figure was impossi-

bly low but now I know that it is not. Sharing the process of how this was achieved as well as detailing exactly how we built our addition, so that you may have the option of building yours, is what this book is about.

Basic Procedures: Carpentry

The bulk of the work in building an addition is measuring and marking various materials, cutting and then fastening them together. Most of the material is wood in one form or another and cutting is done mainly with a portable power saw and fastening with appropriate nails. These acts are performed repeatedly. The time required to erect the addition and its final appearance will in large measure be determined by the speed and accuracy with which these basic acts are performed.

Sawing

For cutting wood less than $1\frac{1}{2}$ inches thick, I use a $6\frac{1}{2}$-inch (blade diameter) heavy-duty Skil portable electric saw.

For cutting wood $1\frac{1}{2}$ inches or thicker, I use an $8\frac{1}{4}$-inch heavy-duty Skil portable electric saw.

I am naming these specific tools, and all others, for no reason other than because they have performed well for me over long periods. Several manufacturers offer more expensive worm-driven saws that are better mechanically than the two I've mentioned but I've found them unbalanced, heavy, clumsy and was thus obliged to use both hands while making most cuts. The last fact alone ruled out this type of saw since my left hand will be in use while I am making most cuts.

Manufacturer's cheap models should be avoided since they simply don't stand up to the hard use one has to expect in building an addition.

All saws are sold with adequate maintenance instructions and recommendations for types of blades to be used for cutting various materials.

I use a 28-tooth carbide-tipped blade in the $8\frac{1}{4}$-inch Skil saw for all rough work. The teeth of this blade are made of carbide steel and stay sharper many times longer than the chrome or other steel alloys used in ordinary blades. The blade costs about $22 versus $3.50 for an ordinary one. It cannot be filed and must be reground when dull but despite this is superior by far to the ordinary blade and well worth the additional cost.

For fine work, I use a plywood blade in the 6½-inch saw. Many lumber yards and hardware stores will exchange a dull blade for a resharpened one for $2.

Although it is not essential, a radial arm saw is an excellent tool to have while building the addition. It will pay for itself in time saved and make all sawing a lot easier. I have used a Sears 12-inch model for more than twenty years and found it adequate for all but furniture-making.

The protractor has a long stationary arm that lies across the board to be cut. The short arm is adjustable from 0 to 45 degrees left or right and the degrees are marked on a semicircular scale. A wing nut on the short arm locks or unlocks the protractor. The end of the wing nut comes to a point and serves as an indicator on the scale. The short arm lies along the far side of the board.

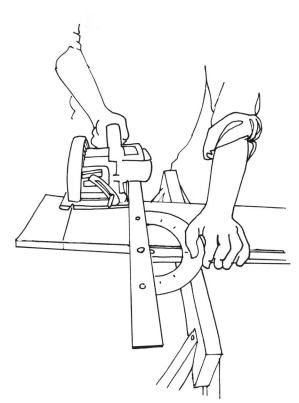

Protractor, board-sawing squarely to exact length

Most often I will be cutting (cutting always means cross-cutting as opposed to ripping) the board at a right angle. I do this by first setting the protractor at 0 degrees. (When first purchasing a protractor and intermittently thereafter, I draw a line across the board with the protractor set at 0, then place a framing square along the line and side of the board to determine whether it is in fact a right angle. If not, I adjust the protractor to the framing square and mark the position of the true right angle on the scale of the protractor.) When the long and short arm form a right angle, I place the protractor on the board, short arm against the far side and long arm across.

I hold the short arm firmly against the board by pressing it toward my body. I place the table of the power saw on the board. The left side of the table lies against the long arm of the protractor. *The blade is back from the wood so that it can rotate freely.* I press the trigger and start the saw.

With light forward pressure, I push the saw through the wood while sliding the side of the table along the side of the long arm. Since the long arm is at a right angle to the board and I am making a parallel cut, the cut will also be at a right angle.

Toward completion of the cut, I push the saw through quickly to prevent the nearly sawed piece from falling of its own weight and tearing a piece of stock with it.

For cutting during rough work, after marking the desired length, I shift the saw and protractor in unison until a tooth of the blade bisects the mark while the rest of the thickness of the blade (kerf) lies on the side of the board that will not be used. I move the saw back so that the blade rotates freely while maintaining the same location with the protractor, and make my cut.

When the power saw is rotating freely, it creates a high-pitched whine. As a cut is begun, it rotates less quickly and the pitch lowers, but if the saw is being operated properly the characteristic whine remains. The whine will be replaced by a flatter-pitched sound as too much stress is placed on the motor and the blade rotates at fewer than desirable revolutions per minute. The optimum speed to make a cut is the most rapid possible without placing undue stress on the motor and one is best able to know when the motor is laboring by the change in sound.

The blade rotates counterclockwise, so that the cut is made from the bottom of the board upward through it. This leaves a smoother surface on the underside. (The reverse is true with a table saw.) In the early stages of construction neither side will be exposed, but a good habit to develop is to mark the side that will eventually be hidden.

A good deal of cutting is done with the board placed on horses. The portion to be cut off should be *free to fall beyond the horses.* When this isn't practical, as in cutting a long board in half, another long board should first be placed under the one to be cut. To the bottom and left of the saw handle is a wing nut. When this is loosened, the saw's table can be raised or lowered and the wing nut tightened when the blade is at the desired depth below the table. I set the depth $1/8$ inch deeper than the thickness of the board to be cut, then make the cut. This leaves a saw mark on the lower board, but it is only $1/8$ inch deep and doesn't prevent the board's later use. I use the same board over and over again in these situations.

When cutting materials such as a 4- × 8-foot sheet of plywood, I first place four 2 ×4s on the floor a foot or so apart and parallel to each other; 8-foot lengths are convenient. (A level patch of ground is an alternative to the floor.) The 2 × 4s serve as a cutting table.

I place the sheet of plywood on top of the 2 × 4s, measure along opposite sides, and pop a chalk line between the marks to indicate where I will cut the sheet. (A chalk line is a spool of string inside a chalk-filled case. The string is stretched taut across the sheet on the marks, raised a few inches, then released so that it leaves a chalk line between the marks. The type with a clip at the end of the string is handiest since one person can use it alone.)

If I am making a cut parallel to the 2 × 4s underneath, I shift a 2 × 4 if it lies in the path of the cut. If I am making a cut across the 2 × 4s, I don't move them.

I set the blade to cut $1/8$ inch deeper than the thickness of the plywood, by lifting the guard, placing the blade against the side of the sheet, and raising or lowering the table as needed. (Much easier than measuring from the table to the tip of the lowest tooth.)

I place the blade at the chalk line. Each tooth is flared in an opposite direction. During the cut, the teeth will remove the width of the flare; $3/16$ inch is usual. I therefore position the blade so that the $3/16$ inch lies on the side of the piece I don't intend using.

At the front of the saw is a U-shaped slot that corresponds roughly to the position of the blade. When the blade lies where I want it, I note the position of the chalk line in relation to the slot and maintain the same position throughout. I watch the slot in relationship to the chalk line and *not the blade.*

I begin my cut from a crouch. (Housemaid's knee is an occupational hazard of carpenters; avoid kneeling whenever possible.) I proceed in a crouch through the entire cut without having to reach too far or contort my body since I can walk on the supported plywood.

While cutting, I am pinching the left front corner of the saw's table with my left index finger and thumb. My index finger is also pressed against the plywood. This helps stabilize the forward path of the saw and keeps it from drifting away from the chalk line. The handle is too distant from where cutting is actually done and control from there is more difficult. Even slight corrective movements from the handle invariably result in much larger ones at the blade and overreaction occurs.

Nailing

For a long time I paid little attention to the type of hammer I used or the way I swung it. This came to an end when I was nailing oak flooring with a 20-ounce hammer that had a steel shaft and rubber grip. In the same room a man I had recently hired was laying three pieces of flooring for every one I did, and doing it with a lot more ease. I knew that I had average speed but had never realized how slow that could be and was both a little embarrassed and miffed. I later studied his swing, but at the time I only noticed that he was using a 2-pound hammer with an ordinary wooden handle and an oversized claw head. I asked to use his hammer. Its greater weight and size made an extraordinary difference in power and accuracy and left me feeling that I had previously been tapping nails with a toy. I offered to buy the hammer. He laughed and gave it to me. I still have that hammer and use it for all nailing.

I grip it at the end of the handle. My thumb goes

completely around and rests on my index finger. If the handle is gripped too hard, a needless strain is placed on the fingers, wrist, and forearm. Gripped too loosely, the handle slides in the palm and blisters result. The force of the grip should be the minimum needed to prevent the handle from sliding when the nail is struck.

A common error is to place the thumb on the handle in order to guide the head. The thumb cannot provide an adequate means of control and the head will rock to one side and cause the user to be inaccurate. To compensate for the poor grip and loss of control, the user shortens the swing to ineffectual tapping.

I use my wrist only to raise the hammer at the beginning of the swing. Another common error occurs at this point when the wrist continues to be used to guide the hammer and provide force for the blow. The wrist is located at the pivot point of the swing, at the center of an arc, and from this location can only deliver a minimum of power. The wrist also has a relatively weak joint and the person using it as a source of power will tire quickly.

Once the hammer has been started upward, no further strain should be felt by either the wrist or forearm. Power in the swing should be provided first by the shoulder and later, when practice has created a facility, by the back and weight of the body—the best sources of the required power.

At the top of the swing the hammer head should be slightly behind the shoulder. As the hammer is brought down on the nail, the weight of the body is added to the force delivered from the back.

Using the 2-pound hammer and a correct swing, two or three blows are sufficient to drive a tenpenny nail and I, of average strength, can nail all day without tiring. (Consider the fact that in building the addition you will probably drive more nails in a day than most people do in a lifetime.)

Once the nail is embedded in the wood with a light tap, the left hand should immediately be removed from the nailing area and placed in the nail apron for another nail. The left hand is superfluous at this moment, and my blackened index fingernail supports this view. I missed the nail and hit my finger instead, which was doubly irritating since there was no reason at all for my left hand to be anywhere near the nail.

When nailing two pieces together, it is useful to start a nail into one of the pieces at an appropriate location and drive it down almost through the wood. This eliminates most of the bouncing about that would otherwise occur.

Another useful technique is to drive the nail through the already stationary member into the member that is loose so that accurate positioning is made easier.

Nails hold least well when driven absolutely straight. A particularly useful type of angled nailing, toenailing, is used often during framing.

I start the nail about an inch up from the end at about a 60-degree angle and drive it down until the head is partially embedded.

The most common difficulty in toenailing of the kind illustrated is that the vertical member bounces about before the nail has entered the horizontal member and stabilized it. One way to reduce the bouncing is to lay the vertical member flat and drive the nails at the 60-degree angle until they are almost through, then position the vertical member on the horizontal one for fastening. This is time-consuming and should be used to familiarize oneself with toenailing, not as a regular practice. By positioning a shoe against the opposite side of the vertical member from where the nailing is to be done, forward movement is prevented. When this isn't effective, the nail is being driven at too shallow an angle.

I don't suppose there's any adult who hasn't nailed something together and in the course of

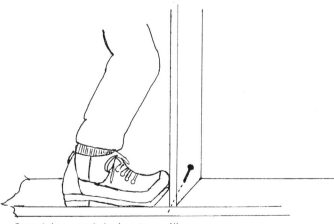

Steadying stud during toenailing

doing it adopted a "technique." If you would like to improve the way you nail by using the technique described, be prepared to misfit nails for a while, but perserverance will pay off in greater effectiveness.

Plumbing

In the past fifteen years or so plumbing has shifted away from the use of threaded pipe to copper pipe and soldered fittings for water lines and DWV (Drain-Waste-Vent) plastic pipe and fittings for drains, waste lines, and vents—a combination that will endure longer than the house and has the added advantage of being far easier to work with than the previous materials. A totally inexperienced person need not have apprehensions about tackling the installation of the bathroom since soldering is the only skill involved and is happily, quickly and easily acquired.

Plumbing work is done in two stages: "roughing in" and "finishing." During the roughing-in stage, hot and cold water pipes are brought from the existing plumbing to the bathtub and basin and a cold water pipe to the toilet. The ends of the pipes are brought beyond the plane of the wall and temporarily capped. Drain pipes are installed for each of the fixtures and are joined into a waste line that in turn is joined to the existing waste line. The drains are continued upward and are joined into a single pipe that continues through the roof (vent).

The finishing stage is begun after the walls and floor are completed (the tub is positioned on the subfloor), and the work involves attaching the fixtures to the previously installed water lines and drains.

To solder, you will need a propane torch , solder, flux, a brush $\frac{1}{4}$ inch or so wide and a few inches long, a sheet of fine emery cloth, and a thick rag dampened by water. The solder should be acid-core and a mixture of lead and tin with a proportion of at least 50 percent tin. The flux (removes impurities created by heat) may be paste or liquid. I've tried many brands of flux and, despite a wide variety of prices, found no difference in quality. A pipe vise, though not essential, will be a great help here and throughout the plumbing work. A chain-type vise capable of holding 3-inch pipe is both cheap and adequate.

Tear a 1-inch-wide strip from a sheet of emery cloth and rub it over the end of a length of $\frac{1}{2}$-inch copper pipe until the metal is shiny for an inch or so. Shine the inside of a copper fitting and push it over the pipe to its shoulder, a narrowed portion of the fitting that limits pipe entry to the optimum distance. Light the torch and restrict the gas flow to obtain a flame about 3 inches long. Warm the pipe and fitting for a few seconds, brush flux completely around the joint and shined surrounding area. Uncoil a few inches of solder and hold the roll in your left hand. Keeping the tip of the torch two inches or so away, direct the flame at the center of the fitting and *not on the pipe*. Shift the flame to all portions of the fitting and avoid remaining on any particular spot. In a few seconds the flux will begin to boil. Continue to shift the flame over the fitting for several more seconds,then place an inch or so of solder on the joint. If the solder doesn't melt, *do not direct the flame at it*. Continue heating all portions of the fitting for another few seconds and apply the solder again. As soon as the heat in the fitting and pipe is sufficient to melt the solder, immediately pull back the flame several inches and keep heating the fitting lightly until the solder that has clumped on top of the joint "runs" around it. Remove the flame and simultaneously deposit an additional inch of solder to the underside of the joint. Wait fifteen seconds or so, then wipe the joint with a damp rag.

When the solder begins to run (spreads rapidly in a ring around the joint), capillary action sucks it into the gap between the fitting and pipe to make a watertight joint.

If the joint has a leak, the most obvious defect will be a lack of solder in portions of the joint. Leaks also occur if impurities have lodged in the solder; they will appear as black specks. These specks should not be confused with dark films that form over the solder due to the flux. The discoloration is normal; leak-producing specks penetrate the solder rather than lie on its surface.

When portions of solder do not adhere, in most instances, too much heat has been applied. To correct the condition, reheat the joint and remove the fitting with pliers. Wipe off excess solder and try again. (Both the pipe and fitting may be reused despite the film of solder that remains on them.) As soon as the solder has melted and *before* it begins to run, move the flame farther back than on the previous attempt and continue to heat the fitting until the solder runs around the joint. A common error is to keep the flame on the fitting as the solder is running. This creates excessive heat and the solder doesn't adhere.

The joint that will not leak has a shiny appearance throughout, and no gaps along its circumference are evidence that the necessary capillary action has occurred.

To test a soldered joint for leaks, cap one end of the pipe and install a ³/₄-inch threaded fitting at the other end. Attach a garden hose and turn on the water. Any large leak will be immediately evident but wait a minimum of fifteen minutes to allow small leaks to show themselves.

During the actual installation, a few leaks may occur. However, all water lines will be tested while the walls are still open and joints accessible. Any leaks discovered are fixed at that time.

Tubing cutter

Copper pipe of various lengths will have to be cut; this is best done with a cutter of the type shown. The pipe is marked at the desired length and the thin cutting disc placed on the mark. The rollers opposite the disc are tightened against the pipe by turning the handle clockwise. The tool is then rotated around the pipe while simultaneously tightening the disc so that it keeps penetrating uncut portions of the pipe wall until it is completely through it.

The DWV pipe and fittings are made of polyvinyl chloride (pvc). (Abs, another type of plastic, is equally good. It is slightly larger than pvc and the two are not interchangeable.) Standard 10-foot lengths and all required fittings are available at any plumbing supply house. Lumber yards also stock pvc pipe and fittings but usually charge more.

Pvc pipe is most easily cut with the tool pictured. It is really a metal-cutting tool but works well on plastic. The pipe cutter is used in the same way as the copper pipe cutter except that the pressure maintained against the pipe is less. If the pipe eases out of the tool during cutting, too much pressure is being exerted. The pipe cutter should be capable of cutting 3-inch pipe, the largest size that will be used.

An alternative to the pipe cutter is a hacksaw. Its use requires a bit more labor. (The hacksaw leaves burrs along the inside of the pipe that are removed by reaming. The burrs become a cause of blockage if not removed.)

To join DWV pipe and fittings, the outer surface of the pipe and inner surface of the fitting are first cleaned with a dry rag. If either is particularly grimy, a special pvc cleaning fluid should be used. Pvc glue is spread with a swab (which comes with the can of glue and is attached to the cap) around the inside of the fitting to its shoulder and around the pipe end for the same distance. (Throughout the

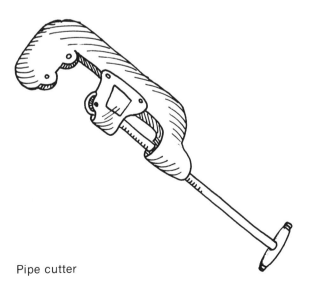

Pipe cutter

plumbing work, assembly is made much easier if the pipe is secured in a vise.) The fitting is then pushed over the end of the pipe to its shoulder and rotated clockwide for $1/8$ turn or so to distribute the glue evenly and seat the fitting. Several minutes should be allowed for the glue to set. Although the joint does not attain maximum strength for several hours, it is strong enough to be handled several minutes after application.

Except for a few instances in which special assemblies are made (these do not require unusual tools or skills), the procedures described are all that are needed for the actual work. The rest is specific information which will be supplied in complete detail in Chapter 7.

Wiring

Parents and teachers caution children about the dangers of electricity and instill a fear of it. This is, of course, legitimate, but the fear continues into adulthood because neither parents nor the educational system removes the fear by providing an understanding of electricity. A great many people shy away from any electrical work despite the fact that it is a basic part of homeowning.

Science has established that electricity is a stream of electrons, the negatively charged particles that orbit the nucleus of the atom. For the sake of efficiency, utility companies that produce electricity transmit it through conductors (wires) at very high pressures or voltages. A cylindrical device mounted on a power pole, a transformer, reduces the voltage to 120 volts for home consumption.

The amount of electricity (the amperage) varies; in newer installations 100 amperes is a minimum amount and 200 amperes usual. As the amperage is increased, the diameter of the wire that will conduct it must also be increased and electrical codes have established the specific relationship: a 200-ampere service requires a 00 copper wire or 0000 aluminum wire. Wire sizes are given as numbers; the smaller the diameter, the larger the number. We will be installing a 20-ampere circuit for the addition and it will require a #12 wire.

A circuit is simply one or more electrical positions controlled by a single circuit breaker or fuse. The circuit breaker is a protective device that shuts off automatically as a result of the excessive heat produced when the amount of electricity conducted through the wire attached to it is too great for the diameter of the wire.

Wattage is another term frequently encountered. It is the amount of electricity consumed and is determined by multiplying the amperage and voltage. The 20-ampere circuit of 120 volts has a theoretical capacity of 2400 watts (less in practice). Electricity is metered and sold by the kilowatt-hour, 1000 watts used for one hour.

Unless your installation is very old, if you look at the wires coming to your house from the power pole, you will see that there are three: two covered by insulation and one bare.

Each of the insulated wires carries 120 volts. (actual voltage varies about 10 percent.) They are called hot or live wires. At a minimum of 14 feet above the ground, the two hot wires are connected to two other wires which in turn become hot. The two wires continue into the meter and are attached to terminals (connecting points) at the sides and top of the meter. At the bottom of the meter are two additional terminals at the sides and wires are connected to them and brought into the main. The meter itself forms the connection between the two sets of wires and provides a continuous path to the main.

The main is a metal box from which the electricity in the entire house is distributed and controlled. It is usually located in a garage or basement but may be placed in any readily accesible area.

The primary means of control in the main is the main circuit breaker that is usually positioned at the top of two metal parallel bars to which the smaller circuit breakers are attached. The amperage rating of the main circuit breaker is marked on it. The main breaker has two terminals and the two hot wires coming from the meter are attached to them. When the switch of the main breaker is on, electricity is fed through the parallel bars to all the smaller circuit breakers mounted on them, and when in the off position, shuts off power to the entire house.

To distinguish the hot wires, the insulation covering them is usually colored black and red but may be any other color except green or white.

The utility company runs one end of the bare wire into the ground (literally) and the other end is attached to a third insulated wire above the house.

This is called the ground or neutral wire. It continues into the meter, is attached to the upper center terminal, and proceeds from another lower center terminal into the main.

At the top of the main is a collection of different-sized terminals, all silver and all joined. This is called the neutral bar and the ground wire (always white) is connected to the largest lug. A bare copper wire is connected to another lug and the other end to the main water pipe. (The pipe must make continuous contact with the earth for at least 20 feet.) When this isn't practical, an alternative is to attach the ground wire to a "driven " ground, a length of metal driven into the ground. The purpose of the ground wire is to conduct spent electricity (electricity that has been used and lost its voltage) into the ground, where it is dispersed.

Both a hot wire and a ground wire are necessary for the 120-volt system, one to supply power and the other to conduct away the "waste." They are never connected to each other, and all such controls as switches or circuit breakers are installed along the path of the hot wire while the ground wire is without interruption.

A 240-volt installation uses only the two hot wires. The ground wire becomes unnecessary since each of the hot wires alternately acts as a ground wire for the other.

Some appliances (such as dryers and stoves) require both 120 and 240 volts, and in this installation both hot wires and the ground wire are used.

Except for a few minutes of work at the very end of installing the 20-ampere circuit for the addition, the wires will contain no electricity whatsoever. The last bit of work in the main will present no hazard if two simple precautions are observed: switch the main breaker off and keep tools away from the terminals of the main breaker where the hot wires from the meter are connected. (It is almost impossible to strike the terminals accidentally since they are located within the body of the main breaker.) By taking these two precautions, no electricity will be present and the simple connection required can be done in complete safety. I have performed the electrical work to be presented a great many times and can assure the novice that he or she will not be unpleasantly surprised by shocks or shorts.

The addition will be a 20-foot square. Electrical codes require that a duplex receptacle (outlet) be installed for every 12 feet of usable wall space. After such items as doors, closets, and so on are subtracted, six outlets in the bedroom and one in the bathroom will be needed.

Assuming normal requirements, one 20-ampere circuit is more than sufficient. If more than a normal requirement is anticipated, an additional circuit can be installed in the manner that will be detailed for the first.

No. 12 Romex-two-wire with ground

The circuit will use a type of wire called flexible nonmetalic sheathed cable, commonly known as Romex. More particularly, the Romex will be two-wire #12 with ground. It will be controlled by a 20-ampere circuit breaker installed in the main.

Romex contains three wires inside an outer sheath of insulation. One wire is covered with black insulation, another with white, and the third wire is bare copper. In the main, the black or hot wire will be attached to the circuit breaker. The white or ground wire will be attached to any unused terminal on the neutral bar. The bare or grounding wire will also be attached to a terminal of the neutral bar. (The bare wire is an added protection against accidental shocks or shorts and is required for safety though it doesn't enter the 120-volt system.)

Romex will be strung from the main to the addition and routed to seven receptacles, two switches, an overhead light in the bedroom, and a wall-mounted light fixture over the basin. The black and white wires will be attached to terminals of receptacles and light fixtures and the black wire alone to light switches. The bare copper wire will be attached to metal boxes in which the receptacles and lights are mounted.

The outer insulation of Romex is most easily removed with a stripping tool that costs under a dollar and is available in any electrical supply house. The stripper is laid around the Romex, pressed shut and pulled back to the end. The sliced outer insulation is peeled back and removed with wire cutters. If care is taken not to cut the wires inside, the outer sheath may be sliced with a sheetrock knife and removed.

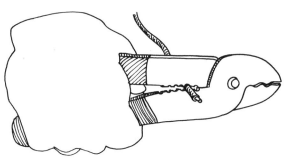

Wire strippers

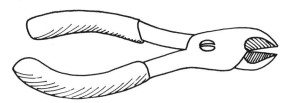

Wire cutters

The above illustration shows wire cutters for cutting both the Romex and its interior wires to length. In order to make connections to terminals, the ends of the black and white wires will have to be stripped of insulation.

This is best done with the pictured wire stripper.

The wire is placed in the hole marked 12, the jaws closed, the handle rotated two half turns, and the wire stripper pulled back. A $^3/_8$-inch length of insulation is what will have to be removed most often; when longer lengths are needed, they will be specified in the course of the work.

The actual electrical work is no more complex than what I have described, and even if you have had no previous experience, you should take this opportunity to rid yourself of a fear that has no place in an adult.

FOUNDATIONS

2

The foundation of an addition is most often the pictured continuous type with crawl space, identical to the foundation used for the house. In this installation a ribbon of concrete 16 inches wide and 8 inches thick, the footing, is poured on the ground between form boards along the perimeter and to a depth below the frost line (the depth to which the ground freezes in any particular locality). A foundation wall of concrete block or poured concrete is then erected on the footing. The interior area of the structure is supported by intermittently spaced piers made of concrete footings and blocks. Wooden girders (sills) are laid on the piers and their ends supported by the foundation walls. Floor joists are nailed at right angles to the tops of the girders and the substructure completed with half-inch sheets of plywood nailed to the joists to form the subfloor. (The same foundation is used for houses with full or partial basements.)

In parts of California, Florida, and the Southwest where ground-freezing is not a factor, the slab, another type of foundation is frequently used. In this installation concrete is poured over the entire floor area and its surface then becomes the subfloor. The slab is as structurally sound as the continuous foundation. (There are other types of foundations, but their use is restricted primarily to summer houses, cabins, and special situations not usually encountered in additions.)

If one examines the drawings of both foundations, it is immediately apparent that the slab uses a lot less material (and labor) than the continuous type. There are no concrete-block foundation walls, no piers, girders, joists, or plywood subfloor. Forms are single boards outlining the perimeter whereas the continuous type requires parallel form boards and additional forms for each pier and concrete blocks erected on them. Because the footings of the continuous type are placed below the frost line, the site has to be excavated to a minimum depth of 18 inches to permit access even when freezing isn't a factor and upward from 32 inches when it is. To pour the slab, only the topsoil need be removed. Translated into money, one can expect to pay a contractor $2500 to build the continuous type and $500 at most for the slab. Since there is no advantage in using one type or the other from a structural viewpoint, the choice of the slab is self-evident for homeowners in non-freezing climates.

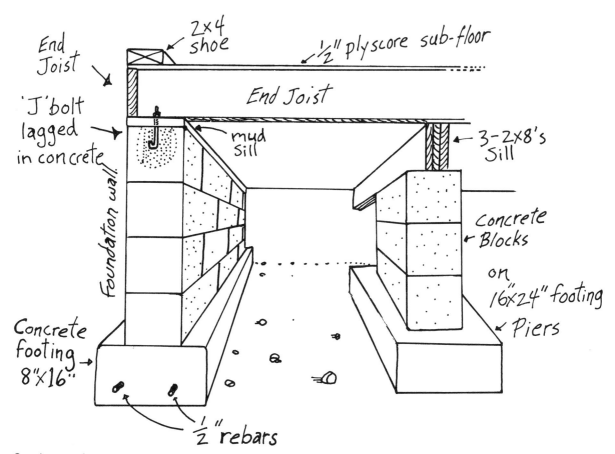

End
Joist

2×4 shoe

½" ply score sub-floor

End Joist

'J'bolt lagged in concrete

mud Sill

3-2×8's Sill

Foundation wall

concrete Blocks

on 16"×24" footing

Piers

Concrete footing 8"×16"

½ "rebars

Continuous foundation with crawl space

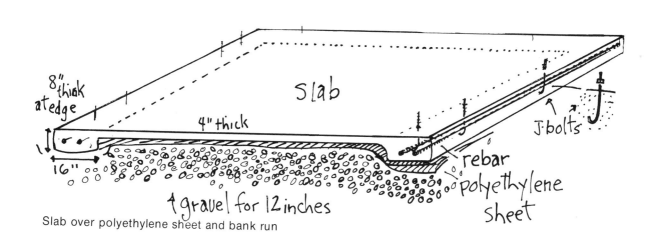

8" thick at edge

Slab

4" thick

J·bolts

16"

rebar

polyethylene Sheet

gravel for 12 inches

Slab over polyethylene sheet and bank run

In regions subject to freezes, the superior choice of the slab is not as evident but will become so once objections to its use are refuted.

A widely held misconception about a slab is that the ground beneath it will freeze and cause the concrete to rise and crack, an action called heaving. Heaving does occur when the slab is poured on a subsoil of sand and clay since this mixture retains water, which freezes, expands, and causes the concrete to shift. However, if material such as gravel is laid under the slab prior to pouring the concrete, no water will be retained and no matter how cold it gets, there is simply no water to freeze. My own house rests on a slab over gravel and in seven years since its construction, no damage whatsoever has occurred despite the fact that it snows frequently and the temperature is well below freezing a good part of the year. (The ground froze to a depth of 5 feet during the past year.)

I have built many homes on slabs in the Northeast and have never had problems. Most often I've used "bank run" as a bed instead of gravel because it was readily available, cheap, and worked well in draining water away under the slab. (Bank run is a type of small stone obtained from river banks.) I once used ground glass that I obtained free from a local waste disposal plant. Any inert, noncompressible material that doesn't absorb water will do equally well as a bed.

Another widespread objection to the use of the slab rests on the belief that the house will always feel damp. This belief is justified if the builder hasn't taken the necessary step to prevent dampness. Concrete absorbs moisture readily and it evaporates in the warmer interior of the structure, creating an uncomfortable feeling. However, if a vapor barrier such as a plastic sheet is laid over the bed before the concrete is poured, it will prevent the slab from absorbing moisture. My belief is based on practice and includes living in a slab-built structure and experiencing the fact.

Another objection is that concrete is a hard surface to walk on. This is indisputable, but one should keep in mind that the slab needn't be the finished floor unless economy is the deciding factor. Every option for a finished floor that exists with a continuous foundation is also available with the slab. In addition, the slab lends itself to the use of masonry materials for the bathroom floor, an optimum installation and one that cannot be used with

the continuous-type unless added support is provided under the subfloor.

A further objection is that slabs develop cracks and cause structural damage even when freezing is not the cause. Sidewalks, roads, and garage floors all serve as a basis for this apprehension since they do develop cracks that are highly visible. One shoud understand that cracks in residential concrete installations occur for three basic reasons: the bed under the concrete was not adequately compacted, exposure to severe climatic changes, and water seepage which carries away portions of the bed supporting the slab. None of these conditions applies to the addition; if a crack develops for other reasons, it will be a long time in coming and of no structural consequence. One should also remember that the addition will be supported by footings that are identical to those used for the continuous type and are more than adequate for any residential structure.

A question that naturally arises is: If the slab is as good as the continuous type in all climates and a fifth the cost, why isn't it used everywhere all the time? A thorough answer would have to describe the evolution of foundations from the early settlers and their use of cellars or basements, an area beyond the scope of this book. For today's homeowner planning an addition, the fact that slabs have been used everywhere for more than fifty years with proven reliability and cheapness is sufficient basis for its use.

Constructing the Slab

After the site and size of the addition have been determined, the height of the slab in relation to the house must be decided upon before work can begin. The slab may be placed so that its finished floor will be level with the house floor or on a lower or higher plane. Less labor is involved if the slab is one or several steps below, since the amount of dirt to be removed will be minimal. However, unless you are preparing the site yourself no savings will be made, because an operator with a backhoe can prepare either site within the usual one-hour minimum. (You should expect to pay $19 per hour for the machine and operator. An additional charge is normally made for moving the machine to your site.)

If you choose to have the addition floor on the

Multiply Your Living Space

same level as the house floor, the first step is to establish the height of the house floor on the exterior wall to be shared with the addition. Using a drill bit long enough to go completely through the wall (6 inches should be enough), bore a hole in the door-to-be area just above the baseboard. Measure the distance from the hole to the floor and mark the same distance down from the hole in the exterior siding. The mark will be used as a height reference for the finished floor of the addition.

The material used to cover the slab can vary in thickness from $3/16$ inch (if vinyl asbestos tile or a similar material is laid directly on the concrete) to as much as 3 inches or more if slate or other kinds of stone are used. A specific selection should be deferred until options in the flooring chapter are examined, but for now let's assume the material is inch-thick maple, the amount I will allow in determining the height–placement of the slab.

The slab will absorb small amounts of humidity that are not nearly enough to make one feel uncomfortable but sufficient to cause wooden floorboards to expand and buckle. It is therefore inadvisable to install maple directly on the concrete, nor will the prior application of tar paper over the concrete surface eliminate the problem. Buckling is avoided by the use of sleepers, construction lumber laid on the slab to which the floorboards are nailed. Sleepers are best installed on edge to create the desirable feature of a relatively larger air space between the concrete and flooring. Sleepers are commonly 2×4s measuring $3 1/2$ inches on their wide sides ($1 1/2$ inches on the narrow sides). (Lumber obtained from a sawmill will measure $3 7/8 \times 1 7/8$ inches.) I will be using 2×4s on edge as sleepers and, combining $3 1/2$ inches with 1 inch thickness for the maple, will place the height of the slab $4 1/2$ inches below the reference mark.

To determine how deep to excavate, I must allow for the thickness of the slab and the bed of bank run beneath it. Along the perimeter, the slab will be 8 inches thick and 16 inches wide and 4 inches everywhere else. The bank-run bed will be 12 inches thick. By combining these amounts with those of the maple and sleepers, it will be necessary to excavate to a depth of $24 1/2$ inches along the footing area and $20 1/2$ inches under the remainder of the slab. Both depths are measured down from the finished-floor reference mark on the siding.

An experienced backhoe operator can prepare the site for $38. If you do it yourself by hand, be prepared for a couple of days of hard work. (If a backhoe is used, have the operator scrape off the topsoil into a separate pile for later reuse.) Several additional feet of excavation on all sides will also be needed for ease in working and handling materials.

If the removal of the topsoil causes a depth lower than needed, additional bank run should be procured to bring the site to the required height.

During excavation, if shale or granite formations are encountered before the required depth is reached, unless the stone is loose no attempt to remove it should be made. The stone should be regarded as a bit of luck since less soil is removed and less bank run needed.

If rock formations are solid and high enough to cause the slab to be less than a minimum concrete thickness of $2 1/2$ inches in any particular place, reduce the bank-run bed partially or totally to achieve the minimum concrete thickness. If more depth is still needed, an additional inch can be gained by using 2×3s on edge in place of 2×4s for sleepers and still another inch by laying the sleepers flat. Rock formations do not retain sufficient water to cause heaving and make an adequate bed.

The footing should be a full 8 inches thick throughout. It is rare to find difficulty in obtaining this thickness. However, if rock formations jut from the ground on the site, unless the rock is shale or loose granite, it is advisable to select an alternate site. The backhoe can clear even boulders without too much trouble, but if the rock is granite and solid, removing even small amounts requires a jackhammer and lots of work. Jutting granite sites should be used only when no viable alternative exists.

After completion of the excavation, the perimeter of the addition is defined by level strings attached to batter boards. The instrument used to accomplish this is a transit level that can be rented for $7 per day, more than enough time to do the needed work even if you haven't a clue about its use. A few minutes of instruction at the rental place will enable you to use the instrument. However, before renting the transit, I would assimilate the procedure for laying out the addition.

The transit level, batter boards, and string procedure to lay out the addition is optimum but not essential, particularly for a relatively small addition. With a bit more time and effort and without the transit level, one can lay out the addition to an acceptable degree of accuracy in the following manner:

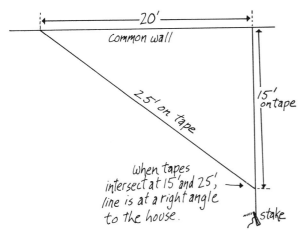

3–4–5 triangle for squaring addition

Using a 4-foot carpenter's level as a reference, pop a level chalk line across the exterior siding 4 1/2 inches down from the mark that indicates where the finished floor is to be. Mark the beginning and end of the 20 foot wall of the addition on the chalk line.

Obtain three 2 × 8s, 20 feet long, taking care to turn them on edge and sight down their lengths to make sure they're straight. The boards are normally a few inches longer than 20 feet and the extra inches will be needed for two of them. Cut the third exactly 20 feet long and set aside for later use.

The width of a 2 × 8 is usually 7 1/2 inches (but it does vary). Tack a scrap of wood to the siding 7 1/2 inches below the chalk line at each end of the wall. Lay one of the 2 × 8s on edge on a cleat in roughly the position it will occupy as a form board. Using the 4-foot level, prop up the other end until the board is roughly level. Mark 15 feet from the siding on the board. Place a tape measure at the beginning of the 20-foot wall and extend it to the board. Shift either the board or the tape so that the 15 foot mark bisects the 25-foot mark on the tape. Drive a stake beside the 20-foot board. Lower or raise the board until the bubble in the 4-foot level is on dead

center. Mark the height of the board on the stake and then nail the board to the stake at the level line. The board is now level and lies at a right angle to the house.

Nail the previously cut 20-foot board to the installed board and prop its opposite end as needed to make it level. Mark 20 feet on the third board; attach one end to the cleat and the other to the second board at the 20-foot mark. Drive a stake on the outside of the right angle made between the two boards, level them with the 4-foot level, and attach to the stake. Since the first board was installed at a right angle and the other boards are of equal length, they will also be at a right angle to each other and the house.

During the nailing of the boards to the stakes, they may have shifted slightly out of level or square and it is advisable now to recheck and readjust as needed.

The 2 × 8s that will serve as form boards for the slab are positioned at a height that will make the finished floor of the addition the same as the finished floor of the house. They are also at a right angle to the house, but small discrepancies inevitably occur when using the 3,4,5 triangle procedure. These can be reduced to a point well within allowable tolerances by measuring the diagonals of the square and shifting the corners slightly until both diagonals are exactly the same length. When this is accomplished, the forms are perfectly square.

Starting from the common wall and proceeding outward, drive stakes into the ground every 4 feet or so and nail through the 2 × 8s into the stakes. Shovel dirt against the outside of the form boards to an inch or so below their tops. The stakes and dirt stabilize the boards and prevent them from bulging when the concrete is poured.

Installing the Drains

Once the form boards are in place but before the bank run bed is deposited, provision must be made to remove waste from the bathroom fixtures. This is accomplished through a drainage system composed of pipes and fittings known as drains. Waste leaves the fixtures through these drains, enters a waste line, and ends up in the existing waste line from where it proceeds to a municipal sewer line or a septic tank.

Multiply Your Living Space

When waste and water flow through the drains, they displace air present in the pipes. If the displaced air has little or no means of escape, the air becomes compressed and exerts a pressure against the flow that either causes it to drain very slowly or stops it completely. To prevent this situation, all fixtures are vented. Each drain and fixture to which it is attached is provided with an additional length of pipe that has an end open to the atmosphere through which the displaced air can escape. For the sake of economy and ease of installation, the vents of the tub and basin are connected to the larger vent of the toilet and displaced air from all three proceeds up the toilet vent through the roof and into the atmosphere.

For similar reasons, the drains of the basin and tub are connected to the bowl drain within as short a distance as practical and the waste from all three fixtures flows in one waste pipe to the existing waste pipe and empties into it.

We will be using 3-inch pvc pipe and fittings for the bowl drain and vent and 1 $^1/_2$-inch pipe and fittings for the basin and tub drains and vents.

(At this point the exterior siding of the entire common wall should be removed as well as the sheathing in the bathroom wall area. I am assuming that this has already been done.)

In order to position the drains and vents in their correct locations, stable references for measuring heights and distances are necessary; these are

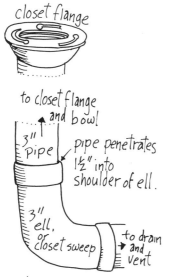

Closet flange, closet sweep and nipples for drainage under bowl

already at hand in the common wall and form board. Since the form board will later have a skeletal 2 × 4 wall beside it, I am allowing 3 $^1/_2$ inches for all measurements made from it. All height distances are made from the chalk line on the common wall that corresponds to the height of the slab.

The center of the bowl drain is 64$^1/_2$ inches from the formboard and 12 inches in from the finished common wall. In non-standard toilets such as "low boys," the distance from the finished wall is 14 inches.

The first drain to install is for the toilet bowl and the first fitting a closet sweep. The sweep is an elbow (ell), and like all ells (unless otherwise specified) turns 90 degrees in direction but does so with a wider-than-ordinary arc. Waste from the bowl makes its first turn at this fitting and less likelihood of blockage exists if the turn is gentle. However, closet sweeps are not "hot items," and if there is difficulty obtaining the fitting an ordinary ell can be substituted and will provide adequate rather than excellent service.

I cut a 30-inch length of 3-inch pipe to be positioned vertically under the bowl outlet. At present it will rise 6 inches or so above the height of the slab but will later be cut as needed. I glue the sweep or elbow to an end of the 3-inch pipe.

In the vise, I glue together the pictured assembly with solvent cement. Its overall length is 12 $^3/_4$ inches from the center of the bowl drain. It is composed of three nipples and three tees with all side outlets of the tees facing upward. The first, a sanitary tee (which has an arced shape to assist drainage), will receive the waste from the tub and is 3 × 3 × 1 $^1/_2$ inches. (The arcs are positioned so that they aim toward the wall.) The second sanitary tee will receive the waste from the basin. The third tee will receive the bowl vent and lies at the wall. I glue the assembly to the ell at the bottom of the bowl drain.

The center of the bowl drain is 64 $^1/_2$ inches from the form board. I position the assembly at this distance and raise or lower it so that the vertical 30-inch pipe is 6 inches or so above the slab height. The vent tee lies against the foundation wall of the house and I mark its circumference on the concrete block butting it.

I now need to cut a hole in the concrete block that will enable me to extend the drain into the

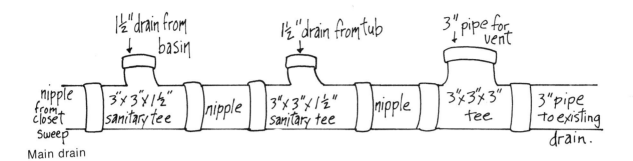

Main drain

basement or crawl space and continue it to the existing drain. I bore a series of holes around the circumference with an impact drill and long (at least 8-inch) carbide-tipped bit. Both the drill and bit can be rented at a nominal cost and will do the job in fifteen minutes at most. I clean out the interior with a hammer and cold chisel. I glue a 12-inch nipple (short length of pipe) to the tee; its end lies in the basement. Using a carpenter's level, I plumb the assembly and wedge it tight with pieces of wood between the nipple and hole. I leave the assembly as is for the time being.

The center of the tub drain lies 79 $\frac{1}{2}$ inches from the form board and in line with the first sanitary tee. I cut a 4-inch nipple of 1 $\frac{1}{2}$-inch pipe and glue an ell to an end. I attach the nipple to the first sanitary tee so that the outlet of the ell faces the tub. I mark 79 $\frac{1}{2}$ inches from the form board on the wall, glue an elbow to a length of 1 $\frac{1}{2}$-inch pipe, place the center of the elbow at the mark, and mark the opposite end at the shoulder of the first ell. I cut the pipe at the mark and attach it to the outlet so that the ell at the tub faces up. I glue a 2-foot-long 1 $\frac{1}{2}$-inch nipple into the outlet. The opposite end of the pipe extends well above the height of the slab. I will trim off the excess later, and install a sanitary tee after the slab is poured and the tub positioned. One outlet of the tee will receive the tub waste and the other outlet will be used for its vent.

Since waste moves through drains by gravity, pipes must be pitched; an $\frac{1}{8}$-to-$\frac{1}{4}$-inch slope for each foot is the optimum amount. The ells being used are actually slightly more than 90 degrees and usually provide the necessary pitch automatically. If necessary, the assembly is flexible enough to obtain the desired pitch by securing the lower end and propping up the end of the pipe closest to the fixture.

To rough in the basin drain, I glue together a 4-inch nipple of 1 $\frac{1}{2}$-inch pipe and ell and attach it to the second sanitary tee with the outlet facing the basin. I measure 24 $\frac{3}{4}$ inches (center of drain) from the form board and mark the distance on the wall. I attach an ell to the end of a length of 1 $\frac{1}{2}$-inch pipe, place the center of the ell at the mark, and mark the opposite end of the pipe at the shoulder of the other ell. I cut the pipe to length and install it with the ell at the basin facing upward. I place a mark 16 inches above the height of the finished floor, glue a sanitary tee to an end of 1 $\frac{1}{2}$-inch pipe, then cut the pipe so that the sanitary tee lies centered on the mark and install it with the arc of the tee facing down. I glue an 8-inch nipple to the side outlet of the tee so that it comes through the plane of the projected wall. The other end of the tee, which faces upward, will be used to continue the vent.

I place a mark on the wall behind the bowl drain 36 inches higher than the projected height of the finished floor. I glue a 3-by-3-by-1 $\frac{1}{2}$-by-1 $\frac{1}{2}$-inch crossfitting to a length of 3-inch pipe and cut the pipe so that the fitting lies just above the mark. I install the pipe end into the tee in the drain that butts the wall so that each side outlet is parallel to the wall. Using 1 $\frac{1}{2}$-inch pipe and an ell, I continue the piping from the outlet left in the basin drain to the side outlet of the cross. I continue the piping from the outlet of the tee in the tub drain and connect it to the opposite side of the cross. At a later time, after the addition has been closed in, I will continue with a 3-inch pipe from the upper outlet of the cross through the roof for 1 foot to complete the venting of all fixtures.

To complete the roughing in, I now return to the 3-inch line in the basement. In all probability, the existing waste line is 4-inch cast iron, and a hole will have to be cut into it so that entry of the plastic 3-inch pipe can be made. I choose a place to make the hole that is closest to the plastic pipe and is also almost horizontal (all the cast-iron waste line will be pitched). I draw a 3 $\frac{1}{2}$-inch circle on top of the cast-iron pipe and cut the hole using an acetylene torch (small oxyacetylene torches being sold will *not* do the job, and if necessary the proper outfit should be rented). Actual cutting time is a few minutes. There are alternate ways of cutting into the cast-iron pipe, but all are much more laborious.

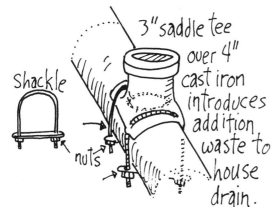

Saddle fitting for cast iron drain of house

I attach the pictured saddle fitting over the cast-iron pipe and tighten it with the two clamps provided.

I continue the 3-inch plastic pipe till I am directly above the fitting with an elbow facing down. Before I make this final connection, I must test the installation for leaks. To do this, I glue thin testing caps over the open ends of all drains. *Using no glue*, I insert a 3-foot length of 3-inch plastic pipe into the outlet of the crossfitting facing upward. I run water from a garden hose into the pipe until full. I wait fifteen minutes or so and check for leaks. They are a rarity, but if a leak is present, I cut out the defective area, add a replacement, and retest. When there are no leaks, I break the lowest test cap and drain the water.

I install the last nipple between the plastic pipe and saddle fitting. The hole in the fitting is a bit larger than the pipe. I fill the gap with a special puttylike compound prepared for use between plastic and cast iron (directions for use are on the can).

I leave the test caps on to keep debris out of the pipes until I am ready to attach the fixtures.

I will bring the hot and cold water lines to the bathroom after the addition is closed in and the skeletal walls of the bathroom have been erected.

I secure the drains with clamps and pipe straps attached to joists in the basement or crawl space and the common wall in the bathroom. I fill the hole in the concrete block around the 3-inch pipe with a mixture of one part cement and three parts sand concrete.

Completing the Slab

To determine the amount of bank run needed, multiply the length and width of the slab and divide by 27. The result will be the number of yards required, cubic yards being the unit of measurement by which it is sold. Cost of the bank run averages $3 per yard delivered. Before it is dumped on the site, remove some and fill under the drains so that they lie solid. Have the driver move his dump truck around the site as he is unloading to distribute the bank run. Pebbles are easily shifted and leveled with a hoe. Leveling can be done by eye, but strings can be stretched between form boards to provide an accurate reference.

After the bank run has been leveled (4 inches lower along the footing area), I spread 4-mil plastic sheets over the entire area and overlap joints for 6 inches or so.

I lay two parallel $\frac{1}{2}$-inch rebars (reinforcing rods) 4 inches apart and 2 inches in from each side in the footing depression around the perimeter. I bend the bars manually to go around the corners and overlap ends 2 feet.

The optimum depth for locating the rebars is $2\frac{3}{4}$ inches above the bottom of the footing. There is no need to wire them in this location. As the concrete is being poured, I lift the rebars to the approximate optimum depth.

To determine the amount of concrete needed for the slab, multiply the length and width of the footing, divide by 27, and divide the result again by $\frac{1}{3}$. Multiply the length and width of the remaining area, divide by 27, and divide again by $\frac{2}{3}$. Combine the two totals to arrive at the cubic yards of concrete needed.

It is advisable to arrange for help to pour the slab. Three people will do but four are better. Several shovels, a rake or hoe, a couple of scrap pieces of

2-foot square $^3/_4$-inch plywood, a wooden float (trowel), and a rectangular steel trowel will all be needed. (The steel trowel can be omitted if the finished flooring will not be placed directly on the slab.)

The preliminary leveling of the concrete will be done with a straight 22-foot-long 2 × 6. Its end will rest on the form boards and the wet concrete will be flattened by slightly diagonal strokes from a person at each end (screeding). The result of screeding is a rippled though flattened surface. The ripple will later be removed with the wooden float.

The process is laborious and can be eliminated through the use of a gasoline-driven screeding machine. A fanlike rotating blade automatically smoothes and levels the concrete as it is moved over the area. The machine rents for $45 per day and will do the job in less than an hour.

Before the concrete has hardened, provision must be made to attach the wooden skeletal framework to the slab. This is done by means of J-bolts, named for the shape. The bolt is $^1/_2$ inch thick and 9 inches long and is threaded at the upper end. They are spaced 8 inches from each corner and every 6 feet thereafter. They are located 1 $^3/_4$ inches in from the form boards and are positioned so that 2 $^1/_2$ inches or so extend above the surface of the slab. J bolts are inserted into the still-wet concrete immediately after screeding is completed.

Ready-mix concrete (it simply doesn't pay to mix it yourself) will remain pliable at least a couple of hours after it is poured; the actual pouring will not take longer than fifteen or twenty minutes at most. There is no need to rush about, and since the work is hard one should do it at a pace slower than normal.

Ready-mix trucks are equipped with a movable chute, and one person should be assigned the job of guiding the chute to unfilled areas. If the chute is not long enough to reach a particular spot, have the driver move the truck closer to it. Ready-mix companies allow an hour for pouring their load without an additional charge; this amount of time is far more than necessary for an addition.

The person handling the chute positions it at the far end of the site and deposits concrete slightly above the height of the form boards in successive bands 2 feet wide or so. The people at each end of the screed board begin their slightly diagonal strokes at the form board parallel to the common wall. The fourth person, using a rake, shifts excess concrete to shallow spots. The entire slab is poured in this manner.

After all the concrete has been dumped and screeded, the screeders return to their initial position and rescreed the entire slab. The person formerly on the chute now begins to trowel the surface with the wooden float, using broad semicircular strokes. The person formerly raking begins to insert the J bolts.

After the second screeding has been completed, squares of plywood are laid on the still-wet concrete, and the screeders trowel the surface flat with wooden floats. (If the weight of the person causes the plywood to sink into the concrete to a depth greater than $^1/_4$ inch, floating is premature and more time should be allowed for the concrete to harden.)

Troweling with a wooden float produces a flat but rough surface. The rough surface is fine if the finished floor will not be laid on it but must be smoothed if it will. Smoothing is accomplished by troweling with the steel trowel, using the same broad semicircular strokes.

If water collects on the surface during troweling, work should be discontinued in the area for ten minutes or so. If troweling is continued, additional water will be brought to the surface and with it cement, the lightest of the materials in the concrete. Cement alone has no structural strength, nor do its particles adhere well to each other. If the concrete is permitted to dry in a watery state at the top, the cement will very soon flake off.

In areas around pipes, screeding is substituted for by hand troweling to achieve a flat surface.

If the weather turns during the pouring of the slab and rain appears possible, cover the entire slab with plastic sheets. Rain will dimple the surface but not otherwise affect the slab. If severe dimpling occurs in any particular area, the depression can be filled with epoxy cement, a type that will adhere as a film. This will not be necessary if the finished floor is not to be laid directly on the surface of the slab.

Allow concrete to set overnight. Although it will take a month or so for the slab to cure completely and achieve maximum strength, it will be strong enough to walk and work on.

FRAMING

—3—

Cutting and assembling the skeletal structure is the framing phase of building. Framing lumber is most often Douglas fir, a type of evergreen logged and milled in the Northwest. It is a strong and reasonably straight wood that is stocked in all lumber yards. Standard lengths begin at 8 feet and increase in multiples of 2 feet to 24 feet. Widths are 2, 3, and 4 inches and increase in multiples of 2 inches to 12 inches. Like all lumber, Douglas fir is sold by the board foot. (A 2 × 6 foot long is one board foot.) At this writing, Douglas fir sells for around $350 for 1000 board feet.

Colonial settlers did not have Douglas fir available and built frameworks of pine, hemlock, fir, chestnut, spruce, and other local woods. Many of these homes, now two hundred years old or more, are still in excellent structural condition. Though Douglas fir is particularly suitable for mass residential use because of its availability in huge quantities, it is by no means the only suitable lumber, and its inflated cost makes it undesirable.

Of the many suitable substitutes for Douglas fir, hemlock fir and white pine are particularly good. Neither is as strong as Douglas fir, but each will provide a framework far stronger than necessary

and the trees are found in a great many regions. Both pine and hemlock boards are straighter than Douglas fir boards, a particularly welcome asset in cutting and assembling the framework. They do not split as easily during nailing and are lighter and easier to handle. (As a commercial builder, I often find hemlock fir mixed in with Douglas fir and interchange them.)

Thousands of small sawmills scattered throughout the country are the source of alternative lumber. As an example, within a two-hour drive of New York City there are more than fifty sawmills, and I recently purchased hemlock, white pine, and maple for $170 per 1000 board feet from one of them, less than half the retail cost at a lumber yard. One needn't be a contractor or big buyer to obtain the same price, and I could have done as well at any of the other nearby sawmills. If there's a forest in your area (even if you are presently unaware of its existence) there is likely to be a sawmill nearby at which suitable lumber milled from local logs can be obtained at substantial savings.

Lumber from a local sawmill contains too much water to be used immediately. By placing slats of wood between boards being piled (sticking) air is permitted to circulate around each board and lumber will air-dry naturally over a period of several months. As a courtesy, the sawmill will not only deliver your lumber free of charge but stick and stack it as well. Of course, waiting for the lumber to dry is an inconvenience, but since no additional work is required on your part and the savings are substantial, the inconvenience is acceptable.

For a nominal additional charge that varies from 2 to 6 cents a board foot, the lumber can be kiln-dried locally and readied for immediate use.

Sawmill lumber should be planed along either of the 2-inch sides to obtain uniformity of width. This is a usual practice and the sawmill will do it at no extra charge. The remaining three surfaces are unplaned and furry, the normal condition of lumber as it leaves the saw. The unplaned surfaces present no problems in framing, though one must remember that dimensions of 2 × 4s are 1 7/8 by 3 7/8 inches rather than 1 1/2 by 3 1/2 if obtained from a lumber yard. (Other sizes are proportionately larger.) The larger dimensions pose no problem and incidentally provide a heavier and stronger framework.

Although the wooden structural framework is used almost universally in residential construction, it is by no means the only viable option, and masonry walls should also be considered. (The roof framework will be wooden in any case.)

Pictured are five types of wall: all wood, wood and brick, concrete block and brick, concrete block and stone, and wood-stone.

In the all-wood wall, sheets of 1/2-inch plywood are nailed over the outer surface of the 2-×-4

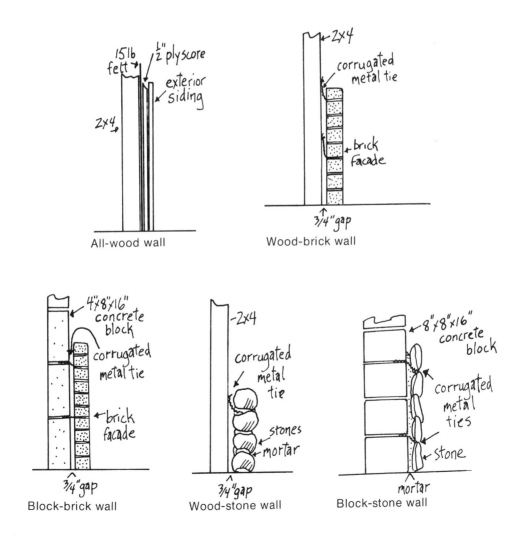

All-wood wall

Wood-brick wall

Block-brick wall

Wood-stone wall

Block-stone wall

skeletal framework and covered with exterior siding. The cost per square foot is 10 cents for the lumber, 25 cents for the plywood, and about 65 cents for a moderately good siding—making a total of approximately $1 per square foot.

Substituting brick for siding, the wood-brick wall would cost $1.25 per square foot.

Substituting 4-by-8-by-16-inch concrete blocks for the wood skeleton and using brick (or a similar masonry material), the cost would also be $1.25 per square foot.

Using 8-by-8-by-16-inch concrete blocks and stone, the cost is 45 cents per square foot.

Using a wood skeleton and stone if it can be obtained free, the cost is 35 cents per square foot.

From this comparison of cost, the choice of a wood-and-stone wall is optimum for economy. This presupposes that the appearance of the stone as an exterior covering of the addition is pleasing.

The notion of working with stone conjures up visions of Old World masons with consummate skill who alone are capable of erecting stone walls, and most people consider themselves totally incapable of performing this work. It is a comment on our mass-production society that this extremely common material rarely appears in a wall in its natural state, and then only as a decorative patch. And yet, stone is a superb material for a wall, one that is *simple* and *easy* to work with. The final irony is that one would be hard pressed to find an area in the entire country where all the stone needed could not be obtained easily and at low or no cost.

I have chosen the wood-stone wall because it is cheapest, easiest to erect, provides an exterior covering that never requires maintenance, and —most importantly—presents an appearance I like.

Before any walls can be erected, it is necessary to become detailed and specific about windows, doors, and all other items to be located in the walls. With respect to costs, only the windows are of major importance and they are likely to be the single most expensive item in the addition if purchased from a lumber yard.

Building codes require that the glass area of windows be at least 10 percent of the wall area of the room. Since there will be only one exit in the bedroom, codes require that the bottoms of sashes, (the movable part of the window) be no more than 42 inches from the finished floor so that the window can also be used as a fire exit.

Unless you wish a floor-to-ceiling window effect or have other decorative purposes in mind, glass areas less than 3 feet from the floor have little use as a source of light or air, are susceptible to breakage, and often wind up being blocked by furniture. They should be kept at or a few inches above a 3-foot height to maximize the window's use and reduce its cost.

Windows must not have any weight on them other than that of their own members. The width of the opening in the wall in which the window is installed is supported with a structural member directly above the window (header). In practical terms, if you have selected a window that is 12 feet wide, the header above it will have to be a double 2 × 12 and—allowing for another member directly above the header, the plate of the wall—the window height will have to end 16 inches below the ceiling. If the window is 10 feet wide, the top of the window can be 14 inches below the ceiling; similarly, the narrower the window, the higher it can go. If the window is 4 feet wide or less, it can be placed 8 inches below the ceiling.

If you choose a window width greater than 12 feet, the structural support needed is not available as a standard item and you must be prepared to spend, at a lumber yard, five or six times more that the cost of standard lumber. This isn't true about sawmills, where the price remains the same no matter how large the board.

It is more economical to choose two larger rather than three smaller windows. It is also advisable to install windows at least 3 feet from corners so they do not diminish the structural strength of the corners and to make best use of the glass for viewing and ventilation.

In the bathroom, it is inadvisable to locate the window in the bathtub area since water seepage is bound to occur and cause rotting of sill and frames. In the plan of the addition here, it will be seen that there is really no option, since only one exterior wall is present. However, even if your addition has more than one exterior wall, the window should be located in a wall away from the tub or other fixtures, since moisture rots the window frame.

Four window types are readily available: double-hung, composed of two sashes that slide up and down; casement, which pivots on a vertical axis; awning, which pivots on a horizontal axis; and gliding, which slides horizontally. The most impractical, the double-hung, is also the most widely used. Even slight warpage or swelling of wood members creates sticking problems and gaps that permit drafts. Problems begin from the moment of installation and are ongoing. The double-hung window should be avoided.

The awning window is most practical, since it will admit as much air as the double-hung although half the size. It also has an added advantage of admitting little or no water if left open during rain. Because of its design, it is impractical to make awning windows in large widths and heights, and large glass areas are obtained by combining relatively small units. This requires additional wooden members (mullions and frames) that obstruct the viewing area—and duplication of frames leads to higher costs.

The gliding window has built-in problems of heat loss and drafts. Since the sashes glide by one another, a gap must be left between them so that the movement remains smooth. In the closed position there is often a gap between the sash at the center stiles or one develops with normal use as weatherstripping becomes worn.

The casement window has all the advantages of the awning type, except for excluding rain. Problems of sticking and drafts are rare. Its design permits the construction of relatively large single units, so that even if two are joined only one frame is necessary. It provides a maximum of air circulation, unobstructed viewing area and admittance of light. The casement window also has the added advantage of lending itself to long rectangular shapes that are pleasing and is my choice.

Once having determined the number, sizes, and locations of windows, one has the option of buying or making them. (See "Windows" - Index) If you intend to buy them, I recommend Andersen windows. I have used them almost exclusively for a great many years with superior results.

One can expect to pay $150 or so for a 6-×-4-foot Andersen casement window. The glass is the welded type that is closed around the perimeter to form two panes with a $3/8$-inch dead-air gap between them. (A larger air space would be more efficient as an insulating factor.) Despite the current focus on insulating walls, floors, and ceiling areas that total about 14 percent of the possible heat loss, *it is the glass that is by far the single most important cause of heat loss*. Although welded

glass is not nearly sufficient to bring heat losses down to an acceptable degree, it does solve part of the problem and should be considered an essential item.

Aluminum- or steel-framed windows are cheaper than wooden ones, but the initial saving is illusory because the metal windows conduct heat from the house and result in higher fuel bills that consume the gain in a few years and then continue to be a needless expense. Andersen windows are made of vinyl-clad wood that does not conduct heat to a significant degree and contributes helpfully to the energy-saving effort. The wood is also pressure-treated chemically to prevent warpage, swelling, or rotting.

Commercial casement windows are manufactured in many different sizes and their exact dimensions are given in catalogues at lumber yards. A wide variety of ways in which single units can be joined is shown, and one can easily find the exact sizes desired or within a couple of inches of it. The exact dimensions of the rough opening (the opening in the wall into which the window will be installed) are also given for each specific window and used in framing the wall.

Doors are manufactured as flush or panel. Interior flush doors have a wooden frame around the perimeter and a stile at 36 inches. The remaining interior area is filled with intermittent corrugated strips and thin plywood glued to the skeleton. Plywood is ordinarily mahogany or birch—less often pine, fir, or other woods. These hollow-core flush doors sell for under $10 and are adequate.

Panel doors are manufactured in a wide variety of styles that can be seen in catalogues at lumber yards. One should expect to pay $22 per door and up.

Panel doors hold up better than flush doors but not to a degree that selection should be based on this fact alone. The choice lies between a panel door that is more expensive but looks better and a flush door that is cheaper and less ornamental.

No matter what choice is made, it is inadvisable to paint the door. Paint is merely a cosmetic and a poor one at that, since it doesn't wash clean despite advertising assertions, is easily marred, requires periodic repainting, and is an ongoing maintenance cost.

A viable alternative to paint is a product called Watco, a mixture of oil and hardeners widely used as a furniture finish. The panel door is prepared for finishing by sanding with successively finer sandpapers, beginning at 80 grit and ending at 200 grit. (Grit numbers correspond to the number of abrasive particles per square inch of paper.) A belt sander is optimum for use with coarser paper and a vibrating sander for finer papers. The final appearance of the door will depend primarily on the quality of the sanding. (For superior results, one can continue the sanding with increasingly fine paper.)

Watco is then rubbed with a cloth on the sanded door and excess liquid wiped off. The result will be a matte finish as durable as those of commercially finished furniture. (If the excess Watco isn't rubbed off, a shine will remain after it has dried.)

Watco (widely available in the West; in New York City at both Janovic Plaza stores) comes with various pigments that act as a stain and color the door without concealing the wood's grain.

The remaining items recessed in walls are minor and will be dealt with as each construction step is taken.

Building the Walls

Walls are either *bearing* (supporting weight) or *partitions*, which simply divide a space and have no weight on them other than their own members. All the exterior walls are considered bearing because the structural members above them and the roofing require their support. The interior walls that form the bathroom and closet will have no weight on them and are partitions.

The drawing shows three basic members of the wall: the shoe, stud, and plate, all made of 2 × 4s. The shoe lies on the slab and is attached to it by the J bolts previously installed in the concrete. The stud rises vertically from the shoe to the underside of the plate and is nailed at the top and bottom. The plate, comprised of two 2 × 4s nailed together, occupies the same relative position as the shoe and forms the top of the wall.

By convention and code, though it results in overbuilding, studs are placed 16 inches apart. Wherever a window or door is to be installed, an opening in the wall must be made and is referred to as the rough opening or r.o. By necessity, studs are omitted in r.o. areas, and to rectify the resulting

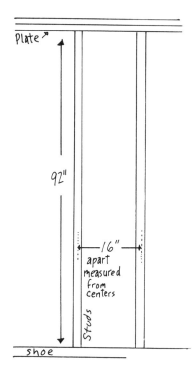

weakness, a member known as a header is installed across the top of the opening which then bears the weight in place of the missing studs.

Pictured is typical framing around windows. The unsupported distance across the width, the span, determines the size of the header. The following formula is used to select header sizes:

SPAN	HEADER SIZE
up to 4'	4 × 4
4'–6'	4 × 6
6 –8'	4 × 8
8 –10	4 × 10
10'–12'	4 × 12

Headers are ordinarily made by nailing together two pieces of the appropriate-sized members and installing them on edge for greater strength than if laid flat. Since the thickness of the skeletal wall is 3 1/2 inches and the header on edge 3 inches, 1/2-inch-thick material is required to bring the header into the same plane as the rest of the wall. This is best done by sandwiching a piece of 1/2-inch plywood between the two members after applying glue and then nailing the header together. Not only does this furr out the header but simultaneously creates one far stronger than the two members alone. (A 4-×-12 header with glued plywood sand-

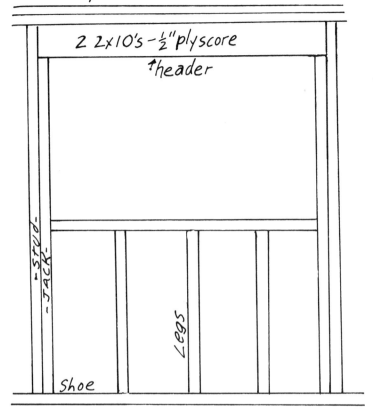

plate

2 2×10's - ½"plyscore
↑header

stud
JACK

Legs

Shoe

Framing for rough opening

wiched between the two 2 × 12s will easily support a span 16 feet long rather than 12 feet if the plywood and glue are omitted.)

Each end of the header rests on a vertical length of 2 × 4 called the jack. The length of the jack is determined by the height at which the window will be placed. Unless the window is wider than 10 feet, an efficient practice is to use 2-×-10 stock for all headers and cut all jacks to a length of 79 inches. The height of the window will then be 13 inches or so below the ceiling and the resulting uniformity will have been accomplished with a minimum of lumber and framing. However, as long as space for the appropriate header is provided, the window can be placed at any height.

When the span of the r.o. is 8 feet or greater, it is advisable to install an additional jack at each end to provide more bearing support for the header ends.

If a hinged or sliding exterior door is being framed, it is advisable to use two studs rather than one on each side of the opening to minimize wall movement if the door is slammed.

In all instances, areas above and below the r.o. are filled in with shorter lengths of 2 × 4s to maintain the 16-inch module, providing bearing strength throughout the wall and a nailing surface for additional material that will be used inside and put over the skeletal wall.

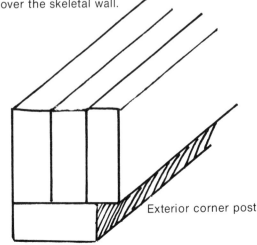

Exterior corner post

To provide adequate strength in corners and nailing surfaces, corner posts are assembled as pictured. Three scraps of 2 × 4 a foot or so long are nailed to a stud at the top, bottom, and center. A second stud is then nailed on top of the scraps. The assembly is turned on its side and a third stud nailed to the 2-inch side.

Galvanized or cement-coated nails are preferable to steel nails in assembling the framework because they hold better. #10 common nails are used to join 2 × 4s on the flat and should be driven at an angle for greater holding power and to keep the tip of the nail from coming through the bottom piece. When nailing through a 2 × 4 into a member that has more than a 2-inch depth, #16 common nails are used. When nailing at a relatively sharp angle, as when attaching the ends of studs to the shoe, #8 common nails are used.

Before the three bearing walls around the perimeter are erected, the fourth wall that is already present and shared between the house and addition should be dealt with. (The optimum time is just prior to installing the drains.) The common wall is covered with siding and a decision about its use has to be made. It can of course be retained and become the finished wall of the addition. If the siding is to be retained, no work on it is necessary at this point.

If the siding is not to be used, it can be removed in several ways. The one that involves the least amount of work but is a little tricky to do is to draw the entire gable outline on the siding with chalk lines. The outline should be 1/2 inch greater on the sides and 1 1/2 inches along the roof. If the siding is metal, a metal-cutting composition blade should be used in the portable saw to cut along the lines. The depth of the blade should be set 1/8 inch deeper than the thickness of the siding. Once the cuts are made, the siding that lies within the addition is removed by first prying loose the top most piece. Nails or clips holding the piece of siding below are then exposed and easily removed. In this same manner all the siding can be removed intact except for the small triangular piece at the very top. For the time being, the siding outside the addition is left as is.

If the siding is wood, a carbide-tipped blade should be used, since it is likely that nails will be struck as the outline is being cut. Every now and then a tooth of the blade will be knocked off after striking a nail, but this hazard is superior to using an ordinary blade that will have to be replaced very quickly—and one is likely to run through half a dozen or more blades before the cutting is completed. (Teeth of carbide blades are brazed back at a nominal cost.)

If the siding is asbestos shingles, no attempt to save them should be made. They should be broken with a hammer and removed.

If you are uncertain about your ability to either mark or cut the outline with precision, the alternative is to remove all the siding as previously described (starting with the topmost piece). During the removal of nails the upper edge of the siding is likely to become chewed up a bit, but these spots will be hidden when the siding outside the addition is resawed and reinstalled after the addition has been completed.

Fifteen-pound felt tar paper is ordinarily used directly behind the siding. If it isn't present, tar paper should be stapled over the entire common wall to keep out rain while the addition is being built.

Pictured are the three bearing walls to be erected and the placement of their members. Walls are numbered for easier identification. The slab will now become a work area and materials not required for walls should be moved away. To keep from cluttering the work area, it is best to cut, assemble, and erect one wall at a time. I will begin wall No. 1.

I pop chalk lines around the perimeter of the slab, each of which measures 20 feet, and then measure the diagonals of the square (the line made by the existing common wall is the fourth side). Previous measurements allowed for minor errors, and if the diagonals do not measure exactly alike I mark the points at which they do and pop additional lines between them. The time taken now to do this will avoid a good deal of needless work later if the structure isn't square.

I cut a 2 × 4 to a length of 20 feet and place the shoe-to-be on the slab and against the bolts. One end lies at the common wall and the other end at the intersecting chalk lines. I place the arm of a square along the side of the 2 × 4 and tongue against the side of the bolt. I draw a line across the 2 × 4, shift the square to the opposite side of the bolt, and draw a parallel line. I measure the distance between the center of the bolt and the chalk

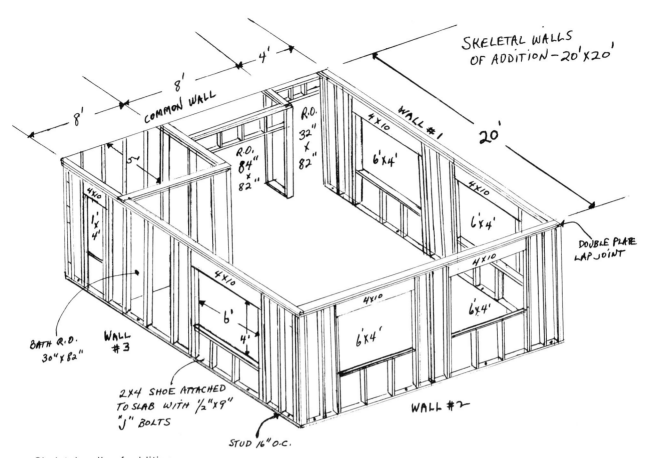

Skeletal walls of addition

line and mark the same distance at the center of the parallel lines to obtain the center of the hole I will bore and also enable the shoe to lie at the chalk line. I maintain the 2 × 4 in the same position and in a similar manner mark off the position of holes to bore for all the bolts.

I place the shoe on scraps of 2 × 4s and bore ³/₄-inch holes, using a ¹/₂-inch drill that turns at 575 rpm. This type of drill is by far the best for boring holes in wood. A Greenlee spur bit is far and away the best to use. Although the bolts are half an inch in diameter, I make the hole slightly larger so that I can shift the shoe if needed to place it continuously at the chalk line and thereby attain a straight wall. I secure the shoe to the slab with washers and nuts, tightening the nuts until the washer is indented into the wood and flush with its surface.

I cut a second 2 × 4 20 feet long; this will be used as the lower half of the plate. I lay it on the slab beside the shoe and tack it to the shoe intermittently to remove curves and align both pieces through-

out their lengths. Standing on the slab and starting at the common wall, I mark 16, 32, and 47 ¹/₄ inches, placing an X to the right of each. I will be placing studs on the Xs and at the marks. Using a square, I extend the marks into lines across both the shoe and plate and place corresponding Xs on the plate. I begin measuring again from 47 ¹/₄ inches, mark off multiples of 16 inches to the end of the shoe, and extend all the marks into lines across both shoe and plate.

The placement of a stud at 47 ¹/₄ inches causes sides of the first and second pieces of plywood sheathing to fall midway on the 2-inch side of the stud and a nailing surface for both is provided.

The drawing of the addition shows that there will be two windows in wall No. 1, each 6 feet wide by 4 feet high, and three equidistant wall areas 2 feet 8 inches in width. The center of the r.o. for the first window is 5 feet 8 inches from the common wall. I mark this distance on the shoe and mark 3 feet outward in both directions. On my left and to the left of the mark, I place a *J* for jack and an *X* for a stud. To the right of the mark on my right, I place a *J* and an *X*. I extend the marks into lines across the shoe and plate and add *X*s. Since jacks do not extend to the plate, there is no need for a mark. I establish the position of the r.o. for the second window in the same way.

I am going to make the windows, and they will be $1/2$ inch smaller in width and height than the 6-by-4-foot r.o. If windows are purchased, the r.o. dimensions should be those given in the manufacturer's catalogue. (The first measurement is always the width.)

If an exterior door is to be installed in the wall, the r.o. should be $3 \frac{1}{2}$ inches larger than the door width and 7 feet high, (measured from the subfloor). If the door frame has an aluminum saddle, the height should be 6 feet 10 inches. The same dimensions are used if a sliding door is to be installed.

If items such as an electric heater or air conditioner are to be recessed in the wall, r.o.s should be procured beforehand and marked.

After marking the shoe and plate for all items in the wall, I detach the plate and place it on edge parallel to the shoe and about 8 feet away.

In standard framing, the stud is 92 inches long. When this length is added to the combined thickness of the shoe and double plate $4 \frac{1}{2}$ inches, the ceiling height will be $1/2$ inch higher than 8 feet (measured from the subfloor). This is an optimum height for installing modular wall coverings, and precut studs 92 inches long can be obtained from lumber yards at no additional cost. However, since we are building on a slab and project $4 \frac{1}{2}$ inches for sleepers and finished flooring, the precut stud will lower the ceiling unnecessarily. It is therefore advisable to use the full 8-foot length of the stud, which will result in a finished ceiling height slightly less than 8 feet.

Cutting studs to exact length is most easily done with a radial-arm saw. One end is trimmed square, placed against a previously positioned stop exactly 8 feet from the blade and the other end trimmed. (The same procedure is used for cutting all members to exact length.) If a radial-arm saw isn't available, the protractor and saw used in unison is a more laborious but viable alternative.

I cut a stud for every *X*. I cut all jacks $1 \frac{1}{2}$ inches

less than the desired height of the r.o. to allow for placement on the shoe. I nail all jack to studs. I place an 8-foot stud on edge, one end against the shoe. I butt the plate to the other end of the stud and drive two #16 common nails through the plate and into the end of the stud. During nailing, the bolted shoe acts as a stop and makes driving nails easier. I nail all studs and jack-studs to the plate in the same manner.

I assemble a header 75 inches long to allow for its continuation beyond the r.o. width for $1 \frac{1}{2}$ inches on each side. I place the header in position and secure it with 16 nails driven through the studs into its ends. I drive additional nails every foot through the plate into the top of the header. I install the second header in the same manner.

I measure down 4 feet from the bottom of the header and place marks on each jack. I cut a 2×4 to a length of 6 feet and install it at the marks by toenailing through the jacks into each end. This member is the subsill. I install another in the second r.o.

I start at the $47 \frac{1}{4}$-inch mark from the common wall and mark the shoe and subsill in 16-inch multiples. (After the wall is up, I will cut short pieces and install them between the subsill and shoe.)

I have been using 2-$\times$-10 stock for headers, butting their upper sides against the bottom of the plate. 2-$\times$-6 stock is adequate for the 6-foot span but if used, a gap will remain between the header and plate that will have to be filled with 2×4s to maintain the 16-inch module. 2×10s work out better despite the fact that they are larger than necessary.

I omit using a corner post for the time being at the end that butts the common wall and attach one at the opposite end of the wall by nailing through the plate into the end of the post. I drive additional nails at an angle upward from the post into the plate.

I cut a 2×4 19 feet $8 \frac{1}{2}$ inches long that will become the upper half of the plate. I flush the ends of lower and upper halves at the common wall and nail them together using 10 common nails spaced a foot apart. The gap of $3 \frac{1}{2}$ inches left in the upper half of the plate at the far end permits the top half of the plate of the intersecting wall to extend into the gap and create a lap joint that strengthens the corner much better than simple butting and nailing.

Beginning at the common wall, I mark off multiples of 2 feet along the entire length of the top of the plate. These marks will later be used to position ceiling joists and rafters.

Before the assembled wall is raised, provision must be made to keep it erect temporarily, and this is done through braces. At approximately 5, 10, and 15 feet and at the far corner, I attach a 2 × 4 to the upper end of a stud with a single nail. Using overly thick nails designed for use with concrete, I nail cleats to the slab at the same distances and about 6 feet or so away from the shoe. In the far corner, I will use the shoe as a cleat. I attach the single stud to the common wall as a brace. (When concrete is less than thirty days old, nails can be driven into it without problems of breaking or bending.)

Three people are needed to raise and secure the wall comfortably on a calm day and four if it is windy. Two are positioned a few feet in from the ends and a third at midpoint. Each person cups his hands around the plate and begins to lift and simultaneously slide the wall until the ends of studs butt against the shoe. When the wall has been raised to waist height, the hand position should be changed so palms are pressed against the plate and the wall raised further by pushing. The wall is then pushed *slowly* upward to an erect position while maintaining the stud ends against the shoe. (An exuberant helper whom I neglected to caution pushed the wall strongly enough to send it toppling over.)

When the wall is erect, two people maintain it in an upright position. The third person nails the single stud to the shoe, places a 4-foot level at its side, plumbs it, and nails the stud to the common wall. The same person goes to the opposite corner, nails the corner post to the shoe, plumbs it, and nails the brace to the shoe. The same person then nails a stud to the shoe that has a brace attached, plumbs the stud, and nails the brace to a corresponding cleat. All three people now nail the ends of studs to the shoe, plumb the wall intermittently at each brace, and attach the braces to cleats.

Wall No. 2 is erected in a similar manner, with the following exceptions. The lower half of the plate is cut 3 1/2 inches shorter than 20 feet and butts the corner post of wall No. 1. The 2 × 4 nailed to the side of the post, the return stud, lies under the lower plate and provides a nailing surface. The upper half of the plate, also cut 3 1/2 inches shorter than

20 feet, extends into the gap left by the shortened upper plate of the first wall and is nailed to form a lap joint. The opposite end has a gap of 3 1/2 inches for the upper half of the third wall's plate.

The third wall is similarly installed, with the following exceptions: A 5-foot length of 2 × 4 is nailed on top of the lower plate with an end butted to the common wall. A gap of 3 1/2 inches is then left to permit entry of the bathroom partition plate that will intersect at that point. At the opposite end of the gap, the upper plate is continuous to the corner.

I nail three intermittently spaced 2-×-4 blocks to the single stud nailed to the common wall, then nail an additional stud over the blocks and repeat the same on the other side.

I cut short lengths of 2 × 4s to fit under the subsills and nail them to the subsills and shoe.

I pop chalk lines to outline the 5-by-8-foot bathroom. Since I am using the full 8-foot length of studs, although not required for partitions, I will also use a double plate for the bathroom interior walls to avoid excessive waste. I build the walls exactly as if they were bearing walls and, because I am not securing the shoe with bolts, nail the shoe to the ends of the studs before raising the wall. I shift the wall so that the 3 1/2-inch extension of the top plate fits into the gap of wall No. 3, align the shoe with the chalk line, and nail through the shoe into the concrete.

The r.o. for the bathroom doorway is 2 inches wider than the door width and 82 inches high.

The closet is framed in the same manner. The r.o. is 2 inches greater than the combined widths of the doors and 82 inches high.

If material such as wood paneling is to be used, nailing surfaces provided by the shoe and plate are insufficient. Even with the best grade of paneling one cannot hope to obtain boards all perfectly straight and a nailing surface midway along the length of the boards must be provided (cats), so that when the curved board is straightened, it can be maintained in that position. Cats are installed by popping chalk lines at a height of 4 feet on the walls, cutting 2 × 4s 14 1/2 inches long, starting nails through the studs, and fastening the cats by driving the started nails into their ends. Cats should be installed alternately above and below the chalk line for easier nailing through the studs.

Ceiling and Roof Framing

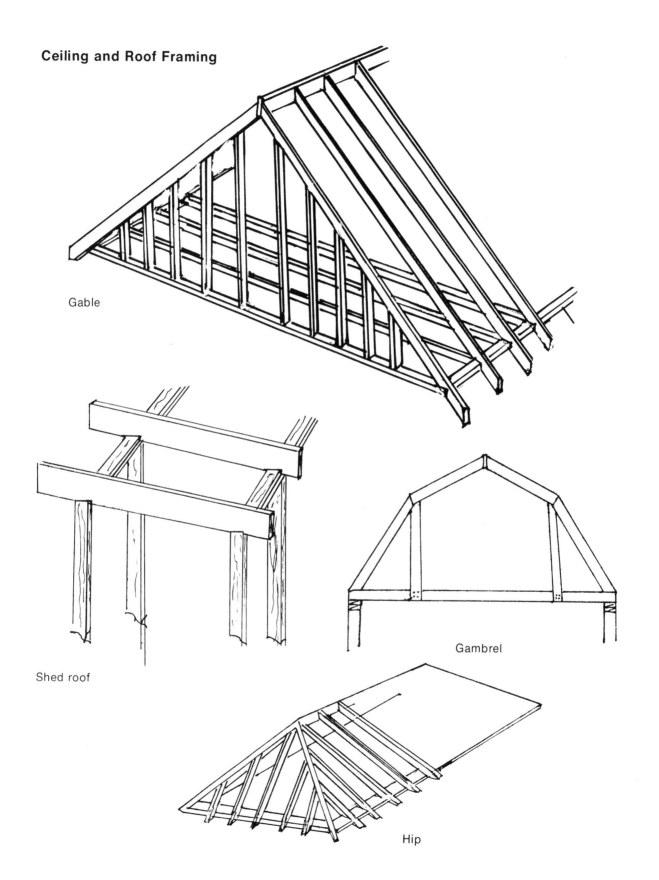

Gable

Shed roof

Gambrel

Hip

Pictured are five of the commonest ceiling and roof structures that can be used for an addition.

The flat roof involves the least amount of material and labor for the skeleton but ends up being the most expensive because it requires a "built-up" or "hot" roof, the most expensive kind. In a hot-roof installation, melted tar is mopped on the roof deck and tar paper applied over it to form a ply. Successive applications of hot tar and tar paper build plies of a hot roof. Three plies is a minimum but four or more are common. Despite its high cost, a hot roof on a *flat* installation is *likely* to develop leaks and will certainly develop them in regions subject to snow and ice. My own negative experiences with flat roofs and those of builder friends have convinced me that the flat roof is totally inappropriate for either residential or commercial construction.

Another roof pictured is the shed. In this type one bearing wall is higher than the opposite bearing wall. When rafters are installed on top of the walls, a slope is created to permit water runoff. The rafters also maintain the bearing walls in a plumb position by acting as tie beams and are also ceiling joists that provide nailing surfaces for the finished ceiling material. By combining three functions in one piece of lumber, the shed uses the least amount of material and labor of all roof types.

By constructing the higher wall at different heights, different slopes can be obtained. The minimum slope should not be less than 3/4 inch to the foot, or water will puddle on the roofing surface and be a source of leaks. The maximum slope should not be greater than 3 1/2 inches to the foot because the roofing material ordinarily used, split sheet, pulls away from the nails holding it.

The force created by weight on a shed roof is primarily downward and rafter sizes are greater than any other type of sloped roof. The size of of the rafter is determined by the span:

SPAN	RAFTER SIZE
8'	2 × 6
10'	2 × 8
12'	2 × 10
14'	2 × 12

The sizes given are those for areas where snow and ice loads are estimated at 30 pounds per square foot, and are correspondingly larger or smaller depending on the projected loads. (Local building departments incorporate the snow load into their codes and will provide the figure.)

Once the span is greater than 14 feet, as in the case of our addition, nonstandard rafters larger than 2 × 12s will have to be used. Nonstandard lumber is several times as expensive as standard lumber and if used, very little or no savings will be obtained compared to other roofs.

The gable roof, with its inverted V shape, is the most prevalent type of roof. It rises from a low point on two exterior walls to a high point, the ridge, usually located at the center of the structure. (The ridge need not be at the center, as in the salt box type.) The shape, however, is not the only factor that determines the type; if two shed structures are butted on their high sides to create the inverted V shape, the result is still a shed roof.

The other element is slope. I will be using 4 inches to the foot slope for the addition, a decision based on appearance alone and one that has no structural advantage over steeper slopes. At 4 inches to the foot, the weight of the roof exerts a downward and outward force in roughly the same degree, and rafter sizes are smaller compared to shed rafters. As the slope becomes steeper, the downward force decreases and even lighter rafters are adequate. For slopes of 4 and 5 inches to the foot, 2-×-6 rafters are sufficient and for steeper slopes, 2 × 4s. In areas of little or no snow load, 2 × 4s are used for all slopes.

The outward force exerted by the roof load will spread the bearing walls outward from their tops unless held upright by an additional member called a tie beam. Tie beams are usually nailed to the tops of the bearing walls and rafters and, since wood will not stretch, maintain the walls in a plumb position as the outward force attempts to spread them. A 2 × 4 would be sufficient for use as a tie beam but is not a good practice because the tie beam also acts as a ceiling joist and over a 20-foot span will sag of its own weight—even more so after ceiling material is nailed to it. It will also bounce about excessively as ceiling material is being installed and make the work needlessly difficult. A 2 × 6 is the smallest size that should be used for the tie beam–ceiling joist.

Although tie beams are best located with their ends directly on the bearing walls, they also fulfill their function if nailed to opposite rafters, as pictured. In this position, the ceiling is raised to 9 feet and its flat surface broken by slanted areas around

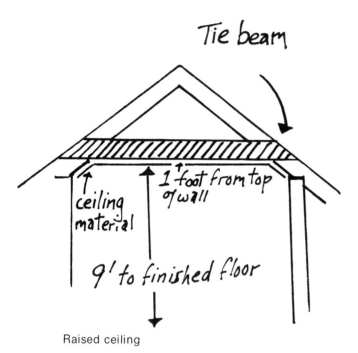

Tie beam

1 foot from top of wall

ceiling material

9' to finished floor

Raised ceiling

impaired. In practice, I have had walls spread when tie beams were placed well below the maximum, and I would position them no higher than 2 feet above the walls.

Trusses have been employed in construction for a long time but their widespread use in residential framing is a late and welcome arrival. The pictured W truss is typical and highly suitable for the addition. Joints are butted and members held together by metal strips at the front and back of each joint, pressed into the wood by machine. Since 2 × 4s are used throughout and fewer members required than for standard framing, trusses use less lumber. They are assembled on the ground rather than at the top of the structure and require a good deal less work. The truss is also stronger than traditional skeletons and is my choice for the addition.

Trusses may be made on the site or purchased from a lumber yard. The pictured 20-foot truss costs $18, which includes delivery to the site and placing it on the bearing walls. (Longer trusses are slightly more expensive.) Ten will be needed, costing $180. (The eleventh is made from 2 × 4s nailed to the common wall.) The cost of materials for making the trusses is about $40. At least two people are needed to raise and install them. I prefer to make the trusses and will detail their fabrication later in the chapter.

The hip roof begins as a gable but the ridge ends

the perimeter. There is a minor additional cost for material and labor but if the appearance is pleasing, the effort is worth making.

Theoretically, a tie beam can be positioned upward from the tops of the walls for $1/3$ the length of the rafter before its structural function begins to be

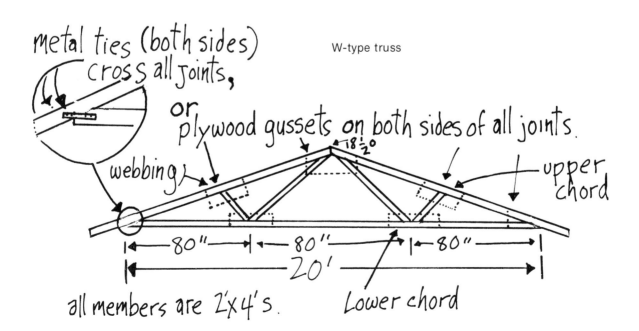

metal ties (both sides) cross all joints,

or plywood gussets on both sides of all joints.

webbing

$18\frac{1}{2}°$

upper chord

W-type truss

all members are 2"x4's.

Lower chord

80"   80"   80"

20'

at the point where the same rafters being used extend downward to the center of wall No. 2. Diagonal rafters are installed from the ridge to each corner. Jack rafters spaced 16 inches apart are then installed between the diagonal rafters and the three bearing walls. Materials are a bit more than the gable roof and an additional day of labor is involved in framing and roofing. These factors are minor and the decision to use the hip roof should be based on whether the shape is the most pleasing.

Keep in mind that the steeper the slope of the roof, the greater the amount of roofing material required. If the slope is steeper than 5 inches to a foot, walking on it is precarious and roof jacks (shelflike metal devices) will be required. Unless one intends to use the attic frequently and desires a large one or if an aesthetic judgment has been made about steep slopes, the use of four inches per foot is the most economical and simplest to install.

If trusses are not going to be used, I begin the standard framing by cutting ten 2 × 6s to a length of 20 feet for use as ceiling joists.

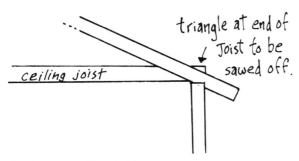

End cut of ceiling joist

I trim the ends as pictured to keep them from extending upward into the plane of the roof. I nail joists to the tops of walls No. 1 and No. 3 at the previously marked 2-foot intervals. I pop a chalk line on the common wall that corresponds to the underside of the joists and nail 2-×-4 scraps along the line to provide a nailing surface for the ends of ceiling material. For the same reason, I nail 2-×-4 scraps on the flat on top of wall No. 2 so that 1 1/2 inches extend into the room.

The traditional way of laying out a rafter is with the use of a steel square but it is quicker, simpler, and more accurate to do it as pictured. I mark 10

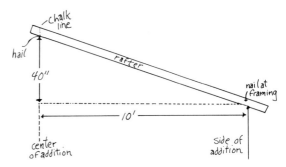

Laying out addition rafter

feet on the shoe of wall No. 2, its midpoint. I extend the mark into a vertical line with a 4-foot level and drive a #16 common nail at a height of 40 inches. (At a rise of 4 inches for each foot, the rafter will be 40 inches higher at midpoint.) I drive a second nail at the corner between the slab and shoe and lay a length of 2 × 6 on the nails so that at least one foot extends beyond the wall at the lower end and a couple of inches at the higher end. I mark the upper end to correspond with the vertical line and the lower end to the intersecting wall (No. 1). I remove the 2 × 6 and position the protractor at 18 1/2 degrees, the angle required to make plumb cuts. I move the top mark back 3/4 inch to allow for half the thickness of the ridgeboard and draw a line across the 2 × 6 with the protractor. I do the same at the lower mark. I measure down an additional foot for the eave and draw a third parallel line.

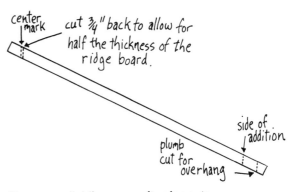

Three parallel lines on rafter for cuts

I trim the rafter along the lines at the top and bottom.

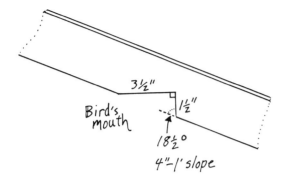

Bird's mouth cut

In order to have the rafter sit fully on the wall with sufficient bearing surface, the pictured triangular piece, the bird's mouth, will have to be cut away. I make the cuts partially with a portable saw and complete them with a sabre saw.

Almost any rafter for any type of roof can quickly and easily be made using the same procedure. For example, if the slope is 5 inches to a foot, the nail at the center is placed at a height of 50 inches. If the span was 16 feet rather than 20 feet, the vertical line would be marked at 8 rather than 10 feet.

To assemble the previously pictured truss, I lay three sheets of plywood end to end on a flat surface. I mark the given dimensions and pop chalk lines between the marks to define each member. I cut 2 × 4s to correspond to the chalk lines. The trusses are identical; since ten will be needed, I cut ten individual members at the same time.

I assemble the loose members so that each lies in its correct position along the chalk lines and attach gang-nailed metallic strips (manufactured for this purpose) over each joint. I turn the truss over and gang-nail additional metal strips over each joint. (A helper is needed in turning the truss over.)

To erect the truss, a helper and I raise one end and place it on top of a wall. Using two ladders, we raise the other end on top of the opposite wall and allow the peak to swing downward (as it wants to do). We repeat this until all the trusses are up and leave enough space to swing them into an upright position. With an additional helper on a stepladder at the center and a person at each end, we rotate the truss into an upright position, push it against the common wall, and mark its outline. We slide the truss to the first 2-foot mark and nail the ends to the plates. The truss must still be held upright.

I nail scraps of 2 × 4 to the common wall along the triangular outline to serve as nailing surfaces for the roof deck and ceiling. I mark off 2-foot intervals on a length of 1-inch stock and nail an end to the top of the cleat on the common wall a few inches from the peak. I shift the truss so that it lies at the first 2-foot mark and tack it there. Similarly, we position all trusses and tack them to successive 2-foot marks. (The board holding the truss erect is temporary and will be removed when the roof-decking material reaches it.)

I use the truss as a model to cut two additional 2-×-6 rafters that will later be used for the gable overhang.

Sheathing

Sheathing is the material applied to the exterior of the wall framework and has a primary purpose of stabilizing the structure. Although sheathing is not essential, it provides many desirable features and is most useful in making the addition tight, free of drafts and leaks, and preventing heat loss. Plyscore, the cheapest type of plywood, is the material used most often for sheathing. (It is also used for the roof deck and subfloor.) Half-inch-thick plyscore is standard and is manufactured in both three and five plies held together by exterior-type glue and, supposedly, plies will not separate if exposed to the weather for six months or so. (I've had ply separation occur within a week of installation.) The simplest way of coping with this problem is to close in the addition as quickly as possible, but since this may not be feasible it is best to use the five-ply type exclusively since separation doesn't occur as often or quickly as with the three-ply. (I've had best results with Weyerhauser plyscore.)

The price of plyscore has risen steeply in the past few years and it is currently selling at $7.50 for a 4-by-8-foot sheet. To cope with this exorbitant price, builders have begun to use plyscore only around the corners. This is sufficient to stabilize the structure adequately and leave the remaining areas free for the use of less expensive sheathing such as exterior sheetrock, exterior particle board, asphalt-coated fiber sheets, and other suitable products. Substitute products are a quarter to half the cost of plyscore and provide a significant saving *without compromising the structural integrity of the addition.*

The roof sheathing (roof deck) requires a material strong enough to support a 2-foot span of relatively heavy roofing as well as snow and ice. Most substitutes for wall sheathing are not strong enough to use on roofs, and those that are, are more expensive than plyscore. Aspenwood, a Canadian roof-deck material available in the United States, is an exception but is still fairly expensive. The best alternative to plyscore on the roof is either secondhand lumber or 1-inch stock obtained from a sawmill. At a cost of 17 cents per board foot, sawmill lumber is the optimum choice and provides a strong roof deck at a saving of 7 cents per foot.

Installing Sheathing

I drive a #10 common nail between the shoe and slab at 6 feet and 42 inches approximately from the common wall. I stand a sheet of plyscore on the nails, long side up. My hands are free and I use #7 common nails spaced every 8 to 10 inches to attach the sheet to all members of the skeletal wall. Since a stud is located at 47 $\frac{1}{4}$ inches, the side of the sheet falls midway along the 2-inch side of the stud. I install five additional sheets at the corners in the same manner.

As mentioned earlier, a good number of substitute materials are available for use as sheathing over the remaining areas. Any will do, and shopping around for the best buy will determine the choice. One should avoid "insulated" sheathing since it is more expensive and the insulation that will later be installed makes its use redundant. I cover the remaining areas with asphalt-coated fiber sheets or any other cheaper plyscore substitute.

The sheathing will have to be cut for all rough openings, but the fit around perimeters needn't be precise and if edges lie $\frac{1}{4}$ inch or so back from the r.o., window casings will hide the unevenness. However, none of the sheathing should intrude into the rough-opening area where it will interfere with the installation of the window.

Installation of Roof Sheathing

Roof sheathing is started at the common wall and lower end of the roof framing. The material may be 1-inch stock from a sawmill (cheaper but more laborious to install) or 4 × 8 sheets of plyscore or an equivalent substitute. The far side of the first sheet should be positioned to fall midway on a rafter. To avoid a concentration of joints on the same rafters, thereby weakening the deck, the second course should be started with the 4-foot scrap that remains after completion of the first course.

Similarly, if individual boards are used, each trimmed end should fall midway on a rafter and accumulation of joints on the same rafter avoided.

Several members will later be added to the lower ends of the rafters and their combined thicknesses will extend the roof line outward 3 inches. For this reason, the first course of sheathing material should be installed so that it lies 3 inches beyond the ends of the rafters. To obtain a straight line and avoid waviness from unequal rafter lengths, it is advisable to measure outward 3 inches from the first and last rafter, stretch a string between the marks, and install the lower side of the sheathing so that it is aligned with the string.

At the gable end (wall No. 2) the sheathing should extend at least 1 foot beyond the wall to provide a roof deck for the eave. After all sheathing has been nailed into position, I pop a chalk line 1 foot out from the wall and trim off the excess to a straight line.

The two additional rafters previously cut (hanging rafters) are ready for installation at the gable end after the roof deck is completed. I start #16 common nails spaced a foot apart in a line $\frac{3}{4}$ inch in from the trimmed edge. With a helper holding one end and I the other, we press the rafter against the underside of the sheathing and align it with the edge. I drive the started nails through the sheathing into the rafter, simultaneously pressing the rafter upward. After a few nails are driven, the rafter can be released and nailing completed. The hanging rafter requires no additional support other than the nails driven through the sheathing.

Scuttle

Access to the attic is provided by a scuttle, a movable portion of the ceiling. Codes require that scuttles be a minimum of 22 by 32 inches. The ceiling joists are already spaced 22 $\frac{1}{2}$ inches apart (inside measurement), and by nailing a couple of 2 × 4s to them 32 inches apart, the rough opening is provided.

Eaves

The portion of the roof that extends beyond the exterior walls is called the eave. The simplest way to deal with eaves is to allow the ends of the rafters to remain exposed and install blocks between them to close the area between the top of the plate and the underside of the roof deck.

After the blocks are installed, silicone caulking is applied around the joints both inside and out. In this eave treatment, members are held to a minimum and a modest amount of material is saved along with a moderate amount of labor. (In this installation, the lower edge of the roof deck is nailed flush with the ends of the rafters.)

Leaving the eave exposed will eventually result in rotting of the roof sheathing along its lower edges. It is not an overnight process and may take twenty-five years or more to occur, but it will happen; slowly in a mild climate and more quickly in northerly areas.

The foot of exposed rafter is not likely to rot, but it will turn gray and black and its ends will split. To prevent an eyesore from developing, both the sheathing and rafters exposed to the weather should be impregnated with exterior Watco. If color is desired, Watco with an appropriate stain should be used. Avoid paint. The treatment will probably have to be repeated every five to seven years or so in rugged climates, less often in mild ones.

Boxing (Closing) In the Eaves

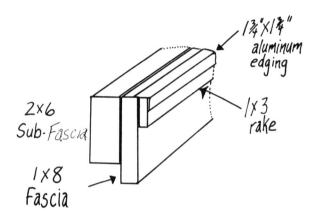

In spite of the additional cost and labor of boxing in the eaves, doing so is cheaper in the long run than leaving them exposed. Maintenance is reduced to mopping on Woodlife (pentachlorophenol) every few years if pine, fir, or a similar wood is used. Redwood doesn't require Woodlife, but redwood oil should be wiped on every couple of years to enhance the appearance.

To box in the eaves, I nail a 2 × 6 to the ends of the rafters, one end butting the common wall and the other flush with the hanging rafter. (This member is the subfascia and is installed on each low side at the front and back of the addition.) I pop a chalk line on the wall to correspond to the lower edge of the subfascia and nail scraps of 2 × 4s at the chalk line. The cleats begin at the common wall and end by butting the hanging rafter. Similarly, I pop on wall No. 2 chalk lines that correspond to the bottom of the 2-×-6 hanging rafters and nail 2-×-4 cleats along the chalk line.

I rip 8-foot lengths of ³/₈-inch plywood to a width of 12 inches or start with 1-by-12-inch boards and nail them to the undersides of the subfascia and cleats. This member is the soffit.

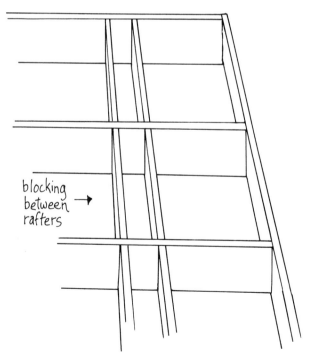

Blocks between rafters along plate

The intersection of soffits at the corners on the gable end leaves a small triangular opening that I close with a similarly shaped piece of stock.

I treat the soffit with natural or stained exterior Watco. Since the soffit is exposed to the weather, I use aluminum ring nails which hold well and do not bleed. (Oxidation causes steel and galvanized nails to rust, which appears as black streaks.) Asbestos shingle nails made from aluminum are readily available as a substitute if ring nails are hard to find.

The fascia, a 1 × 8, is now nailed to the subfascia with its upper edge butting the sheathing and its lower edge below the subfascia. It should also be attached with aluminum nails.

To minimize rainwater falling on the fascia and walls, a member called the rake is nailed to the fascia along its upper edge. Stock for the rake is usually a 1 × 2 or 1 × 3 of the same wood used for the fascia and is finished in the same way.

The rake lies in the path of rainwater coming off the roof and as a means of protecting it, a final member called edging is installed over it. Edging is commonly light-gauge aluminum bent in the center to form a right angle with 1 3/4-inch sides. (To avoid waviness developing in the edging, bend it to form a tighter angle before installation.) The side of the edging that lies on the roof is nailed with roofing nails spaced 1 foot apart; the side over the rake isn't nailed. Edging is installed on the low sides of the roof before the roofing is applied. Along the gable, it is installed after the roofing has been done. Metal edging is cut with a sheetrock knife and joints between lengths lapped an inch or two.

Roofing

The roofing material that actually keeps out the rain may be either wood, masonry, or asphalt.

Wood roofing is almost exclusively cedar shingles. Unlike walls, where 7 inches of each course is left exposed, cedar-shingle roofing requires a 4-inch exposure to prevent leaks and makes an already expensive material even more so. The longevity of cedar-shingled roofs varies a great deal and may be anywhere from seven to twenty years. Successive wetting and drying causes splits and curling that result in leaks before severe deterioration. Cedar shingles are also a dangerous fire hazard, not only to the addition but to nearby

houses since in case of fire shingles may explode off the roof and flaming debris is hurled for long distances. Despite their attractiveness, cedar shingles are singularly inappropriate for use as roofing (their fire hazard has caused them to be outlawed in many areas) due to exorbitant costs, frequency of leaks, and fire danger.

In the masonry category are slate, clay, concrete, and similar products manufactured in the form of shingles. They provide a permanent trouble-free installation and are without doubt the best material for roofs. They are also expensive and often require heavier and more closely spaced rafters because of their weight. The only negative aspect of a masonry roof is its huge cost differential compared to asphalt roofing, which provides a slightly inferior but perfectly acceptable installation. (Slate must be sawn into shingles and holes drilled for attachment.)

Asphalt roofing is a great deal less expensive and requires only standard framing. It is an easy material to install, and an asphalt roof can be expected to last twenty years or more. (The projected longevity is from manufacturers and a rare instance of understatement. Asphalt roofs I installed thirty years ago are still in fair condition.)

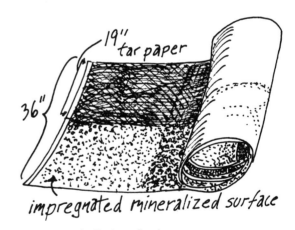

Split sheet (rolled roofing)

Asphalt roofing is manufactured in sheet form as pictured. Sheets are sold in rolls 36 feet long and 36 inches wide (split sheet or rolled roofing). Split sheet is appropriate for use only on roofs with a slope between 3/4 inch and 3 1/2 inches per foot.

The basic material of split sheet is heavy tar

paper. Roughly 18 inches is impregnated with small gravel-like particles to resist the eroding effect of rain. The impregnated half remains exposed. The other half of the split sheet is simply tar paper and is hidden under the exposed surface of the course above it. Split sheet is the cheapest of all suitable roofing materials and the easiest and quickest to install.

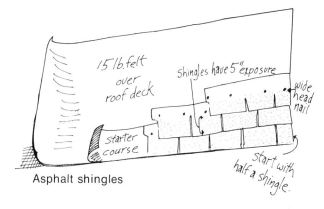

Asphalt shingles

Asphalt roofing is also manufactured in the form of shingles, as pictured. It is widely available in various weights and sizes. In general, the heavier the weight of the shingle, the longer-lasting it will be. The standard size is 2 by 1 foot. Asphalt shingles are appropriate for use on roofs with a minimum slope of 3 1/2 inches per foot and all steeper slopes, including A frames. If used on slopes that are less than the minimum, there is a likelihood that wind will drive rain under them and leaks will develop.

Split sheet at a cost of 10 cents per square foot of roof area (compared to 65 cents or so for masonry and cedar shingles) is available in a limited number of colors. Since white reflects heat rather than absorbing it as darker colors do, it is the best choice from a practical point of view but the color is only a minor factor, particularly since the entire attic will be adequately insulated.

Asphalt shingles at 15 cents per square foot of roof area are the most widely used roofing material and are available in many weights, shapes, and colors. Lumber yards carry catalogues from which a selection can be made. My own preference is the random tab with tan color that looks a great deal

like cedar shingles when installed but is without their negative features.

Flashing

Before roofing is installed, the joint between the roof of the addition and the common wall is dealt with to prevent leaks. This is accomplished through the use of flashing, a metal strip applied to the roof deck and the common wall sheathing over the entire length of the joint. The material most commonly used is aluminum. Standard aluminum flashing is 14 inches wide and sold by the roll or foot.

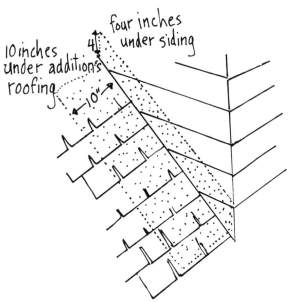

Placement of flashing

I cut the flashing with tin snips a couple of inches longer than the joint, then pop a chalk line along its length at 4 inches. I lay a 2 × 4 at the chalk line and manually bend the flashing to a rough right angle. I tap a piece of 2 × 4 against the partial crease and use another 2 × 4 to obtain a sharp line. I position the flashing with 10 inches on the roof deck and the remainder on the common wall sheathing and nail along the edges with wide-head roofing nails. The excess length lies at the peak. I slit it and fold it over the peak and nail the edges. I repeat this along the opposite side of the gable and fold the excess over the flashing at the peak.

Installing Split Sheet

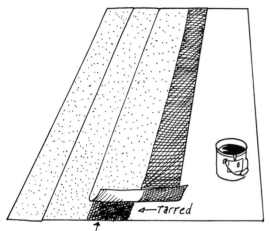

←Tarred

↑
mineralized surface
cover tar paper portion of sheet

Split sheet installed

Unwind a roll of split sheet along the lower edge of the roof deck and trim it roughly to length by cutting along the back with a sheetrock knife. Shift the lower edge of the sheet so that it lies 1/4 inch or so beyond the metal edging. Secure the sheet with wide-head roofing nails driven through the upper half (smooth part) along a line 2 inches and 10 inches back from the mineralized surface. Nails should be spaced 1 foot apart. *Do not* nail through the flashing. Trim the excess from the sheet so that it lies flush with the rake along the gable end.

Unroll a second sheet, align its lower edge with a chalk line (factory-made) marked on the first sheet and nail the upper half. Install each successive sheet in the same manner until the final sheet can be folded over the ridge and nailed. (The sheets needn't be continuous. If two or more pieces are used in one course, each joint should be lapped 18 inches.)

With at least two helpers positioned along the length of the sheet, fold back the gravel surface and expose the smooth nailed portion. The fold should not be sharp or a tear may develop, and particular care should be taken on a cold day since the tendency to tear is greatest when the material is cold and least pliable.

After all sheets have been rolled back, position three 5-gallon cans of roofing cement (also called plastic or cold tar) at the ends and center of the second course. Dump tar globs intermittently and spread them with a notched trowel completely over the black surface. Move the cans to the third course and fold back the first. (If the day is windy, instead of dumping from the can, use a scrap of 1 × 4 to remove tar from the can.)

Walk over the first course and remove bumps or bubbles by sliding your feet toward the downward side. Lift the end of the sheet at the common wall and apply tar under it and over the flashing. Do not nail the final sheet folded over the peak. Use tar alone to attach it. The balance of the roof is installed in the same manner.

Along the gable, nail the roofing to the rake, using roofing nails spaced every 8 inches or so and install the edging over it. Nail the lower edges of the roofing every 8 inches or so through the gravel surface, edging beneath it and into the rake. This completes the roof.

Windows

About 80 percent of the heat loss in an average home is through the windows. More particularly, the glass itself, often comprising 10 percent or more of the room area, is the major factor. Significant amounts of heat are also lost by drafts through gaps between sash and around the frame and rough opening. In recent years the situation has been worsened by the large swing to aluminum and steel windows, resulting in even further heat loss by conduction through the metal frame. We are all aware of the need for energy conservation but unfortunately—through misinformation and plain hustling—attention has been erroneously focused on insulating walls, ceilings, and floors. Most homes built in the past thirty years have been adequately insulated as a standard practice and in homes with no insulation the most one can hope to save is 15 percent of the heat loss and less if the structure is tight. The energy required to produce the unnecessary additional insulation being stuffed into walls, floors, and ceilings is far more than what is saved and no significant progress in energy conservation for the home can be made until the focus is shifted to the glass and window as a whole.

Multiply Your Living Space

Shortly after World War II, storm windows were introduced on a mass scale to cope with heat loss and discomfort. Storm windows, if tightly fitted, diminish heat loss by about 40 percent. However, they are needlessly expensive in requiring two frames, awkward to operate, and frequently require removal in spring and reinstallation in fall. They have a deserved reputation for being eyesores.

The better manufacturers of windows cope with heat loss through the use of welded glass and achieve a reduction of about 30 percent if the dead-air space between the panes is ³/₄ inch and a bit less if ³/₈ inch. Since welded glass is fitted in the sash, only one frame is required and results in less material and installation costs. There are no storage, cleaning or maintenance but, like storm win-

dows, they do not reduce heat loss to an acceptable degree.

In alpine regions of many European countries, heat loss through windows has been reduced to an acceptable degree through the use of triple glazing: three separate panes of ordinary single-strength glass with air spaces between them. Triple glazing has proved to be effective—but unfortunately windows in these countries employ large stiles, gap-producing joints, and incredibily cumbersome and expensive hardware to operate the sash, a design hardly worth copying.

At the present time no manufacturer offers triple-glazed windows at a cost that even remotely resembles a practical possibility. On those occasions that I have used triple-glazing, I was obliged

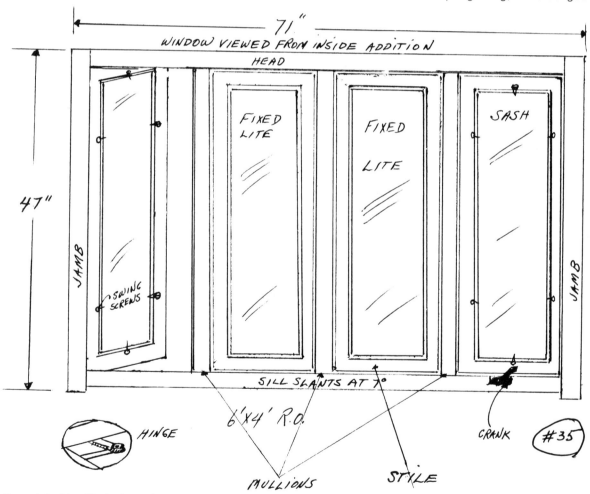

Complete 6' x 4' window with all dimensions

to build the windows myself. *They work well and reduce heat loss effectively.*

Many people consider building windows far-fetched and beyond their capacity, and yet, with a few ordinary hand tools and either a router or table or radial-arm saw, windows can be built by anyone willing to make the effort. Not only will triple-glazing reduce heat loss to an acceptable degree and lower fuel bills, but materials will cost about $30 for a 6-by-4-foot window, a fifth the cost of one manufactured with welded glass that is only 30 percent efficient.

Window frames are exposed to the weather and should be made from materials that will not deteriorate, warp, or be a good conductor of heat. Redwood fits these requirements, as do red tidewater cypress and red cedar. All three woods are soft and easily worked, but their softness is also a liability and care must be taken when working with them to avoid splintering and scarring. Clear white pine is also suitable but should be soaked in Woodlife and finished with oil and hardeners immediately after fabrication and every couple of years afterward.

In designing windows, it should be kept in mind that making the sash requires additional hardware and materials, and additional labor for installation. Movable parts of the window should be restricted to what is needed and in all but the most southerly climates, if only half the window area is sash, more than adequate air circulation will occur.

One should also keep in mind that hardware to operate the sash will also be exposed to the weather and only nonrusting materials such as brass, stainless steel, anodized aluminum (nonanodized will pit) or plastic should be used. (Beware of materials described as rust-resistant.)

The drawing details one of the windows I have built for my addition. It measures 1 inch less in width and height than its r.o. of 6 feet by 4 feet. The smaller dimensions enable me to use standard 12-foot lengths and hold waste to a minimum.

A sash is located at each end of the window; the two center sections are fixed lights. All glass is single-strength, purchased by the case for economy. Wooden members are kiln-dried white pine soaked in Woodlife and finished with clear exterior Watco.

The appearance of the window conforms to my taste and the window you design should conform to yours. I would not hesitate changing its size or shape but advise using only suggested materials and procedures.

The standard method of fabricating windows on the site involves the extensive use of the router and is relatively laborious. A newer and easier method is now possible through the recent development of a fastening device that is a superior offspring of the ordinary wood screw.

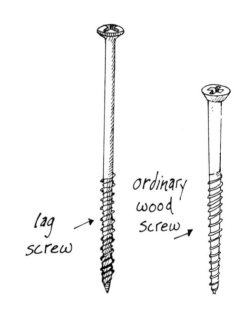

The new screw has alternately higher and lower threads and an extended conical tip brought to a sharp point. The design enables the screw to hold extremely well even when fastened into the end grain of wood, something the ordinary wood screw will not do. Because of this advance, it is now feasible to eliminate all joints formerly required to hold the frame or sash together. For example, when the four stiles that comprise the sash are being assembled, the ends of the horizontal pieces are butted at right angles to the vertical pieces and there was no satisfactory way to secure them other than milling a joint. The new lag screws eliminate the need for a milled joint since they will hold a butted joint securely as pictured.

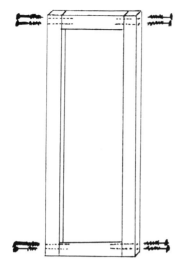

Butt sash stiles secured with two lag screws at each joint

Two screws in each joint are more than adequate to draw the stiles together tightly and securely and milling joints is redundant. (I tried to pull apart the pictured joint with all my strength but was unsuccessful.)

In fabricating the window, I will be using plastic resin glue during the assembly of all butt joints with lag screws.

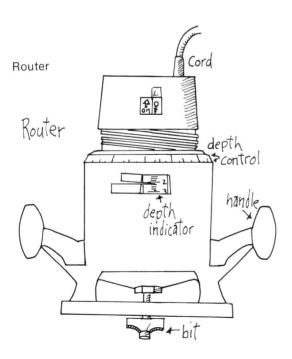

Although the use of lag screws eliminates a good deal of milling, it does not do so entirely, and some joints will have to be cut. This is best done with a router. The pictured router is manufactured by the Stanley Company (Model H 260 A, 9 amps) and is rated at 1 ½ horsepower. I used it for the milling needed to build the windows and found its performance only adequate. It is in the lower price range of the Stanley line, $65. Unfortunately, more powerful routers that perform with excellence are several times as expensive. However, since the wood being cut is soft, it will do the job. (I have used routers of equivalent power made by other manufacturers and found their performance about the same. I would avoid all routers less powerful because they simply won't do the required work.)

The router is electrically operated and has a shaft speed of 22,000 rpm. A chuck lies at the base of the shaft to hold the bit, a piece of shaped metal that actually does the cutting. (A variety of differently shaped bits are manufactured for use with the router and the cut made depends on the particular shape of the bit.) Bits are made of steel or steel with carbide-steel tips. The carbide-tipped bits provide clean cuts over much longer periods than those of plain steel. Steel bits should be avoided since they become dull very quickly and perform in a totally unsatisfactory manner.

To install a bit in the router, a hexagonal nut directly above the chuck is turned counterclockwise until the jaws in the chuck are loose. The shaft of the bit is then inserted fully between the jaws and the nut turned clockwise till tight. (A wrench to do this is always provided with the router.)

To raise the bit after it has been tightened, the arm at the top of the base and on the back is loosened by turning counterclockwise. A large yellow ring at the top of the base is graduated into 1/64-inch marks and further subdivided into marks of 1/256 inch. As the ring is turned clockwise, it lowers the base. Less of the bit extends below the base and results in a shallower cut. To lower the bit and cut more deeply, the ring is turned counterclockwise, the base pushed up against the ring, and the locking arm tightened to maintain the position of the base. The amount the bit is raised or lowered can be precisely regulated by noting how much the ring is moved past a stationary arrow located on the front of the base. For example, if the ring is turned clockwise from a ¹/₆₄-inch mark to the next, the bit will cut ¹/₆₄ inch less deeply than it would have in its former position.

In practice, I approximate the needed depth of the bit by eye and make a test cut into a scrap of wood. I measure the depth of the cut with the brass extension of a folding ruler and then raise or lower the bit the amount required by turning the ring.

Near the top at the back of the router is a yellow switch with *on* and *off* positions marked beneath it. A third position is indicated by an arrow pointing up to the switch. When the switch is depressed and raised, it pops forward into a slot above the off position and locks the shaft, a convenience for changing bits since the hex nut can be turned with a single wrench.

Before moving the switch laterally to the on position, *care must be taken to make sure that the bit is not against any material and can rotate freely*, and I have developed the habit of resting no more than 1 inch of the base on the material to be cut. When first using the tool, I took the added precaution of looking at the bit to make sure it would rotate freely.

The router cuts from any direction with equal results. The base should lie flat on the work; it makes no difference whether the back or front is facing the operator or if the position is shifted during a cut. The router may be pulled toward the operator or pushed forward except at the ends of cuts, when it should be pulled into the work to avoid tearing the stock by pushing to complete the cut.

When cutting parallel to the grain, less stress is placed on the motor than cutting across the grain and should be done faster.

After one has turned on the machine and allowed the bit to reach maximum speed, the bit will slow down as it enters the wood. (This is particularly true of underpowered routers.) If one pushes the router ahead more rapidly and with greater force, the bit will slow down even more and within a very short time overheat the insulation on the armature and trip a breaker. (An acrid smell will result.) Excessive speed also reduces the rpm of the bit below its optimum cutting speed, causing the cut to be chewed up (chunks of wood are ripped out rather than cut away) and reduces the life of the router considerably.

If one cuts too slowly, the bit will heat up excessively and leave black burn marks. Cutting too slowly is also the single most widespread cause of dulling bits prematurely.

When the bit spins freely, it creates a high-pitched whine. The pitch of the whine will lower as the bit begins to cut, but this change in sound should not be dramatic. There is an optimum working speed and the whine that corresponds to it is heard as the bit first enters the wood. Maintaining the same sound is the best way to keep the bit rotating at optimum speed.

The router is not a dangerous tool but can easily become one if attention wanders as it is being used. A bit which turns at 22,000 rpm deserves the full attention of the operator. I've found that the most dangerous moment is immediately after a cut has been completed. One has a tendency to relax while switching off the machine and lifting it from the work to see the cut that has been made. There is no guard around the bit, which continues to spin for a short time after the router is switched off. At this moment, while the operator is focused on the cut and the bit is still rotating, a collision between the bit and operator is possible and practice has shown that the left hand is the victim. An absolutely safe procedure is to switch off the machine and *allow it to remain on the work until the bit has stopped turning.*

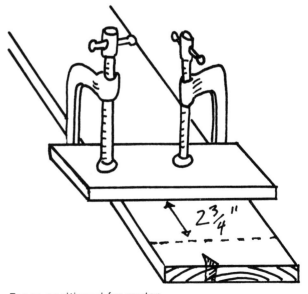

Fence positioned for router

Most often the router will be used in conjunction with a fence (guide) as pictured. The fence may be a straight piece of scrap wood, a carpenter's level, or a similar handy material. The fence is held by C clamps on top of the work and parallel to the cut desired. Since the diameter of the router base is 6 inches, the center of the bit lies exactly 3 inches away. If, for example, I am using a 1/2-inch surface-cutting bit and the fence positioned 2 3/4 inches away and parallel to the desired cutting line, the cut will be made at the desired line. Bits of larger or smaller diameters require adjusted spacing to the fence—using a 3/4-inch bit, the fence would have to be positioned 2 5/8 inches from the desire line, or 2 7/8 inches if the bit is 1/4-inch. In making the cut, the router base is held against the fence and moved along its length. The resulting cut will be straight as the fence.

An excellent feature of the router is that perfectly straight cuts are achieved with no skill required of the operator. However, accurate measuring, marking, and placement of the fence are essential for satisfactory results. In this respect it is better to use a #2 pencil rather than a carpenter's pencil, to obtain a cleaner and thinner line. At the very beginning, it is also advisable to establish a pattern for marking. Mine is to cover the pencil line with the fence so that the line is barely visible. After trimming, the line along the desired cut should also be barely visible; if not, I know immediately that I have done something wrong.

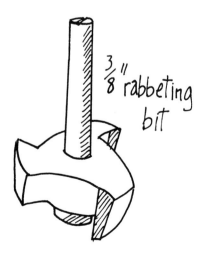

3/8" rabbeting bit

Many bits such as the one pictured have a built-in guide in the form of a wheel over the lower end of the shaft. When the wheel is against the edge of the wood being cut, the cut will automatically extend 3/8 inch laterally and no fence is required. If, for example, a rabbet that is 1/2 inch deep and 3/8 inch wide is desired, the bit is adjusted to cut at a depth of 1/2 inch and the router passed over the work with the guide resting against the edge of the wood throughout the length of the cut.

Unless one is working with a really powerful router (at least 2 1/2 horsepower), the rabbet should be cut in several passes rather than one to prevent overloading the machine.

Building the Window with Butt Joints and Lag Screws

Following are the dimensions for all wood window members:

Jambs of frame, head, and mullions	1 1/4" × 4 3/4"
Sill	1 1/2" × 6 3/4"
Casing (Exterior Trim)	1 1/4" × 2 1/4"
Sash	1 1/2" × 2 1/4"
Stock for rabbets on jambs and head	1/2" × 3"
Stock for sill rabbet	1/2" × 3 1/2"

I apply glue and assemble the head and jambs as pictured, holding them in position temporarily with a furniture clamp. Using a 1/8-inch bit, I bore two holes through the backs of the jambs into the ends of the head to a depth of 2 1/2 inches. (I wrap a piece of tape around the bit at 2 1/2 inches and use it as a depth reference.) The holes are located 1 1/2 inches in from each side and centered on the thickness of the head. I fasten the pieces together with two lag screws at each butt joint and remove the clamp. The screw size is #8 by 3 inches.

The pictured sill is to be installed in a slanted position so that water will run off it. To establish its position, I mark 1 inch up from the bottom of each jamb, set the protractor at 7 degrees, and draw upward slanting lines from the marks. I cut the sill to the pictured shape and dimensions, apply glue, and install it between the jambs so that its underside follows the slanted lines. I maintain the sill in position with a clamp and secure it with two screws in each joint.

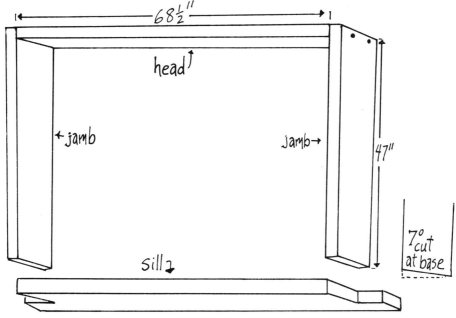

Head and jambs in place

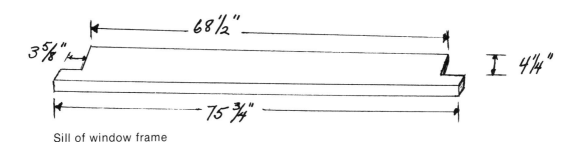

Sill of window frame

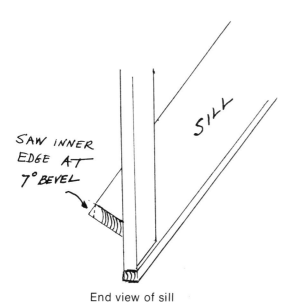

SAW INNER
EDGE AT
7° BEVEL

End view of sill

On the room side, because the sill lies on a slant, its lower edge extends beyond the plane of the frame. It is easiest to make the edge flush by sawing it at a 7-degree bevel before installation, or the excess can now be removed with an electric plane. (The exterior edge of the sill needn't be beveled.)

I mark off the head and sill into four equal sections and install three mullions (vertical members that divide the frame into sections). The upper ends of the mullions are square, their lower ends cut at a 7-degree angle to conform to the slant of the sill. I secure the mullions with screws, two through the head and two through the sill into each end.

The illustration on page 52 shows the rabbet that is formed when $1/2$-inch stock is glued to the wider stock of the head. By gluing additional pieces to the jambs and sill in the same relative positions, the rabbets will be completed. Measuring from the

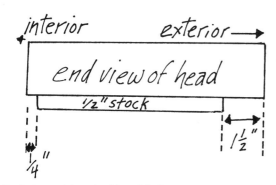

End view of head with rabbet

room side, I draw a parallel line ¼ inch from the edge and continue the lines along the jambs and sill. I measure the distance between the jamb and mullion (now also a jamb), cut ½-by-3-inch stock to that length, apply glue, and secure the piece along the line with C clamps. (For best results, keep the clamps on for at least three hours.) I cut two additional pieces from the same stock and attach them to the jambs. The upper ends of the pieces are square, the lower ends cut to a 7-degree angle. I measure the width between the side pieces and cut ½-by-3 ½-inch stock to that length. I bevel one side of the piece to a 7-degree angle, place the piece on the sill in the position it will occupy, mark its excess width, and trim the second side to a 7-degree bevel. I glue and install the piece on top of the sill.

On the room side, I now have a uniform rabbet ½ inch deep and ¼ inch wide that will later receive a pane of glass. On the exterior side, the rabbet is ½ inch deep and 1 ½ inches wide and will later receive the sash. I create identical rabbets in the same manner in the three remaining sections.

To make a sash, I measure the height between the 1 ½-inch rabbets of the head and sill and cut two stiles ¼ inch shorter than the measurement. These stiles will form the jambs of the sash. I measure the width between the 1 ½-inch rabbets and cut two pieces 4 ⅞ inches less than the measurement. These two pieces will become the top and bottom stiles. (The four pieces are cut shorter to allow for hinges and weatherstripping.) I assemble the four pieces with glue, butt joints, and screws.

Using a ⅜-inch rabbeting bit set to cut ½ inch deep, I run the router around the inner perimeter of the sash on the side that will face the exterior. (The router does not cut in corners and I complete the rabbet in these areas with a wood chisel.) I reset the depth of the bit to cut ¼ inch and rabbet the oppostie side of the sash along the interior perimeter. (This side faces the room.) I cut, assemble, and rabbet the three remaining sashes in the same manner.

I obtain 12-inch × 40-inch single strength glass, place the pane in the rabbeted opening and using the lines of the rabbet as a reference, score the glass cutter previously dipped in kerosene or turpentine. I snap off the excess by seizing it with my fingers and pressing downward and outward. (To avoid the difficulty of trimming small pieces of glass, it is best to make the two required cuts ⅛ inch smaller than the opening.) I run a bead of silicone caulking in the rabbet, press the pane of glass down into it, and wipe off the excess with a putty knife. I secure the glass with small T-shaped pieces of metal called diamond points. The pointed end of the piece is pushed into the wood directly above the glass; half remains over the glass and maintains it in the rabbet. I space three along the length and two across the width. I spread a band of glazier's putty around the perimeter of the pane and shape it into a bevel between the top of the wood and glass with a putty knife.

I cut a second pane ⅛ inch smaller than the opening on the opposite side of the sash (the side facing the room). I obtain stainless-steel U-shaped channel stock and cut it to fit over the perimeter of the pane. The spring action of the channel wedges it securely to the glass.

I mount eight swing screws as pictured and simply turn their arms to lie over the channel and secure the pane in the rabbet. (For convenience, I remove the pane during further work.)

I use the same opening for the screen. To make the screen, I either obtain screen stock or purchase a screen one size larger than the opening. I remove the spline that holds the screening material and disassemble the frame by pulling the four pieces apart. The frame is held together at the corners with right-angled metal pieces that fit into the hollow channel of the framing material. I cut the pieces to size with a hacksaw, trim the screening material and spline with a sheetrock knife, and reassemble.

I bevel the bottom of the sash to a 7-degree angle

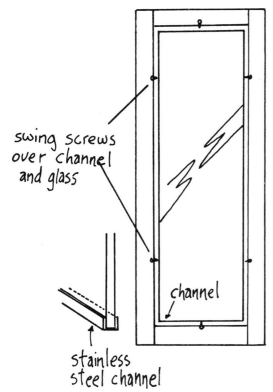

swing screws
over channel
and glass

channel

stainless
steel channel

Swing screws holding glass and U-channel surround

plastic that makes a tight and durable seal. Felt and spring metal weatherstripping are the most common but both should be avoided since they are unsightly, develp snags quickly, lose their seal, and function unsatisfactorily in other respects. To install the T-shaped plastic weatherstripping, cut a groove to receive the vertical part of the T into the 1 1/2-inch side of the sash along its exterior perimeter.

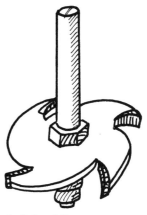

Splining bit

The figure above shows the splining bit that is used to make the groove. Its $1/8$-inch thickness automatically cuts the groove width this amount. The noncutting lower portion of the bit acts as a guide and automatically limits the depth of the groove to $3/4$ inch. The groove should be located at midpoint of the 1 $1/2$-inch stiles and I adjust the depth of the bit so that it will cut at $3/4$ inch. I lay the sash flat and pass the router around the outside perimeter to cut the groove.

to conform to the slope of the sill. This completes one sash, and I build the remaining three in the same manner.

Pictured is one of many kinds of weatherstripping suitable for windows. The material is flexible

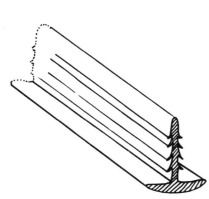

T-shaped plastic weatherstripping

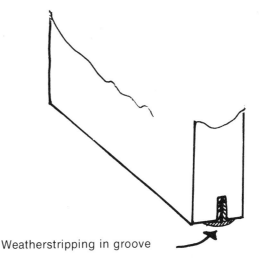

Weatherstripping in groove

I press the vertical portion of the T-shaped weatherstripping into the groove, where it is held by friction, and trim to length.

The sash is now ready for attachment to the frame and hardware for this purpose is needed. The optimum choice is the crank type widely used in commercially built windows. (Adequate installation instructions are contained in the package.) The crank permits the sash to open and close by simple rotation and also locks it in any position. Crank hardware is not yet readily available to the homeowner (the situation is improving) and will probably have to be obtained by ordering it through a lumber yard or hardware store. (The best alternative to the crank is a cumbersome arrangement of piano hinges to swing the sash, a center-pivot friction arm to maintain the sash in open positions, and a handle to manipulate it.) I install the sash with crank hardware in both outside sections.

I lay a bead of caulking in the rabbets of the center sections and press the sash into it. I toenail the fixed lights to the frame with aluminum finishing nails, countersink the heads, and fill with putty.

Using $5/4$-by-2 $1/4$-inch stock, I cut the jambs and head of the casing (exterior trim). The lower ends of the jambs are cut to a 7-degree bevel and butt the sill. Their upper ends are square. Both pieces are positioned $1/8$ inch beyond the edge of the frame jambs and $1/8$ inch above the frame head. The head trim is cut squarely at each end and lies flush with the outside of the jamb trim. I secure the casing to the frame with #10 common nails, countersink the heads, and fill with putty.

I cut two 5-foot strips of tar paper and staple them to the sheathing along each side of the r.o., their excess lengths 6 inches above and below the opening. With a helper, I insert the window into the rough opening. Using a carpenter's level, I shift the window as needed to a plumb and level position. I drive #16 common nails through the trim into the framework to secure the window in the opening. (Nails are necessary only along the jambs and no nailing should be done through the head or sill.)

To prevent leaks from occurring at the joint between the sheathing and back of the head trim, I install the pictured plastic drip cap (available in all lumber yards). The fabrication and installation of the window is now complete.

Exterior Walls

The material chosen to finish exterior walls should not only express one's taste but also fulfill the practical requirement of standing up to the weather with little or no maintenance. Woods that perform well are redwood and red cedar. Neither rots or warps and, left untreated, will gradually turn silver-gray in mild climates. In northerly regions the wood will also turn silver-gray on southerly exposures but blackens facing north and a combination of gray and black elsewhere. The original color can be maintained by swabbing every few years with a mixture of 90 percent Woodlife and 10 percent redwood oil. (For redder hues increase the proportion of oil) The original appearance can also be maintained by using exterior Watco, an oil with hardeners that deposits a fairly durable film over the surface of the wood to resist penetration of the elements.

Wood siding is commonly milled as pictured. It may be obtained in boards of various widths beginning with 1 × 3s, 1 × 4s and increasing in multiples of 2 inches to 12 inches. Beveled siding is installed horizontally; tongue and groove and ship-lap may be installed either vertically or horizontally, or tongue and groove diagonally Allowing for waste and loss of surface exposure due to joints, redwood or cedar will cost about 85 cents per square foot on the wall. Redwood and cedar siding on houses I

Drip cap

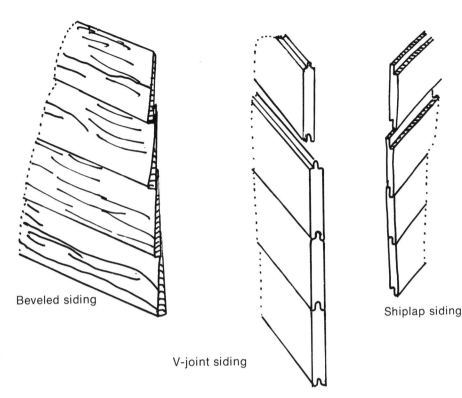

Beveled siding

V-joint siding

Shiplap siding

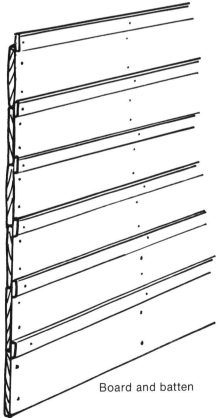

Board and batten

built twenty-five years ago is still in excellent condition but either is simply too expensive today as an optimum choice.

If a wooden exterior is desired, white pine is a less desirable but adequate alternative and will cost about 20 cents per square foot on the wall if purchased from a local sawmill. Boards may be milled into any of the joints mentioned previously or in the pictured arrangement of board and batten. (For cosmetic reasons, the boards may be planed or left rough-sawn.) In this installation the batten is normally a 1 × 2 and the board 6-inch or wider.

If left unplaned and untreated, white pine turns black in a couple of years because of its porosity and becomes an eyesore. It is also highly suscepti-ble to rotting along its lower ends. To prevent discoloration and rotting, Woodlife applied with a sponge mop every two years or so in northerly climates and every three years in gentler climates works well.

If the pine is planed (an additional cost of 2 cents per foot) it will not discolor as readily; it will nevertheless still require treatment though not as frequently.

Multiply Your Living Space

Unlike redwood or cedar, pine warps readily and nailing is done with #8 common aluminum nails. Face-nailed at the bottom, midpoint, and top.

A wooden finish is also provided by 4-by-8-foot sheets of exterior plywood. Plywood of this type is scored vertically to simulate individual boards. Inner plies are usually fir; the outermost ply may be obtained in cedar, fir, pine, and other woods with either a smooth or rough surface. Decorative plywood was formerly significantly cheaper than individual boards, but one can now expect to pay 50 cents per square foot and up. Although exterior plywood is still widely used (mainly for tract houses) and has demonstrated its practicability, it is not an optimum choice because it is expensive and to many people (including me) not very good to look at.

Cedar shingles are another widely used exterior covering. They are available in several grades and types; resquared and rebutted using the best stock and resawn for squareness, ordinary run-of-the-mill, and hand-split. (Hand-split shingles are thicker and larger.) Cedar shingles begin to curl, split, and degrade in a dozen years or so in severe climates. It takes much longer for this to occur in mild climates and thirty years or longer isn't unusual. As a wall covering, 7 inches of the shingle remains exposed. Given its high initial cost plus the fact that only 7 inches of its 18-to-24-inch length is actually covering the wall, cedar shingles are uneconomical and their use justified only by aesthetic considerations.

Aluminum, vinyl, or steel with a baked enamel finish are exterior siding materials that have come into widespread use. All are normally applied horizontally to simulate beveled wooden siding. Costs begin at 60 cents per square foot and rise considerably for better grades and types. Though all stand up well over long periods and require a minimum of maintenance, their high cost rules them out as an optimum choice.

The most widely used and cheapest commercial material for an exterior covering is asbestos shingles. They are easy to install, require no maintenance, and at this writing cost 16 cents per square foot. Look at somebody else's house on which they have been used before you buy.

The most common of all masonry materials used as an exterior covering is brick. The installation is permanent and maintenance-free. Among the wide variety of bricks available, the cheapest obtained from a masonry or lumber yard will cost about 70 cents per square foot. A combination of cost and the ever-present shortage of masons has caused many builders to shy away from brick, but its use for the addition deserves consideration.

Since the exterior walls are already framed in wood, it is not necessary to erect a brick wall (two or more parallel courses joined together) and only a facade (a single course of brick) is needed. The facade halves the number of bricks required and the labor of laying them.

One may use either new or used brick. New brick costs about 13 cents each and used brick 17 to 22 cents. New "used" brick, manufactured to look like old brick, sells for about 15 cents. At these prices, brick is too expensive as an optimum choice but needn't be obtained commercially. I have gone directly to demolition sites many times and purchased used brick for 2 cents each or had them given to me free. Wreckers are glad to get rid of them and homeowners should have no difficulty obtaining used brick at little or no cost. The bricks will have to be transported to the site and cleaned, but this is little enough effort for obtaining a fine exterior finish. (Approximately six bricks are needed for every square foot of wall area to be covered.)

A particularly attractive brick is split-faced limestone manufactured from white cement, sand, and limestone chips. It is made in molds like ordinary concrete blocks and then split along the center to provide a rough and irregular face for each piece. The sides and ends remain smooth. A standard size is 4 by 4 by 16 inches. Split-faced limestone is also manufactured in standard block size and may be used as the bearing wall, eliminating the wood-masonry assembly. The cost will be about the same as commercially obtained brick.

The variety of masonry materials is extensive and a visit to a masonry yard is advisable to acquaint oneself with the numerous options.

My own choice for the exterior walls is stone. It is a superb building material and free for the taking in practically all regions.

Pictured are two kinds of abundant stone particularly suited for the addition. The basalt type, roundish and smooth, relatively hard and dense, is found in fields, stream beds and banks, and other easily reached areas. Stones 4 to 8 inches in diameter are best to work with since each is large

Basalt stone, basalt stone split, shale

enough to fill a respectable area but still light enough to handle easily. Stones can be accumulated over a period of time and stored at the site without fear of deterioration. Only cleaning and wetting are required before use.

The exterior of the basalt stone is gray. It is split with a pickaxe, cold chisel, and 5-pound hammer or a powered impact chisel. The gray color is limited to a thin skin and the interior colors range throughout the spectrum, often containing streaks of metal-bearing ore that add to the visual interest. The installation is also permanent and maintenance-free.

Shale is another type of abundant stone often found as ledges on hillsides after the surrounding soil has been washed away. Natural formations are composed of thin layers. Alternate freezes and thaws usually separate the layers and usable pieces in large numbers are found around the deposit. If necessary, the layers can be separated easily by driving a flat bar into the seam between them. Slate, blue to black in color, is the most common type of shale and may be laid either flat or on edge. The installation is also permanent and maintenance-free.

Stone Exterior Walls: General Information and Basic Procedures

If a masonry wall is chosen, provision for its use must be made before the slab is poured and the footing should be extended 4 inches to support the stone wall. If one is willing to lose 4 inches along each exterior wall, the same 8-by-16-inch footing can be used.

The finished wall will be a solid interconnected mass composed of stones and mortar to fill all gaps between them. Mortar used throughout will consist of 1 part cream (a clay product), 2 parts cement, and 8 parts sand. To this mixture, water is added in the ratio of 30 gallons per cubic yard. (This amount is an approximation and varies in practice.)

Lime can be used in place of cream and is an adequate though less satisfactory substitute. (The amount of lime used is 10 percent of the cement by volume.) *Cream (or lime) is essential for providing necessary workable plasticity to the mortar and markedly better adhesion.*

A practical method of preparing mortar is to dump 2 shovelfuls of cream, 4 of cement, and 16 of sand into a half-bag mixer. The mixer is started and a spray of water from a hose played over the mixture. As soon as material begins to fall of its own weight from the mixing blades, water is stopped and the mixture dumped into a wheelbarrow. The blade of a 10-inch pointed trowel is then run across the surface of the mortar; a smooth unbroken swath indicates that it has a good working consistency.

If the mortar pulls apart during the stroke, not enough water has been added. I add more water and remix with a hoe until I achieve the unbroken swath.

If water seeps out of the mix or collects in hollows, too much is present. I add dry materials proportionately and remix.

In the course of work, water will evaporate and more must be added to maintain the desired consistency. On a hot day one can expect to add water every twenty minutes or so; on a cold day, perhaps every hour. *Consistency of the mortar is the single most important factor* in using masonry materials satisfactorily and maintaining the mortar at the proper consistency, an essential requisite.

Facade masonry walls should be constructed so that a 1/2-to-3/4-inch gap is left between the back of the wall and the sheathing to permit water condensed on the back of the stone or brick to trickle down without wetting the wooden framework. Water collected at the bottom drains through "weep holes," gaps produced by omitting vertical mortar joints periodically along the lowest course (One every three feet).

The facade wall has a width of only one brick or stone and should be supplied with more lateral strength than that provided by the material itself. This is accomplished through the use of a corrugated strip of metal called a tie.

Ties have two predrilled holes at one end. The holes are used for nailing to studs and ties should be installed in each 16 square feet of wall area. The opposite end of the tie is then laid on top of an adjacent brick or stone, mortar deposited over it, and a new brick or stone laid. The ties easily and effectively join the facade to the wooden framework and provide additional lateral stability.

In order for the mortar to adhere to stone (or brick) and provide a satisfactory continuously joined bed, dust and dirt must first be washed off. In addition, the stone should be wet when laid. Dry stone or brick sucks water from the mortar and causes it to harden prematurely. The dried mortar will then be crumbly, adhesion will not have occurred, and the resulting wall will be structurally deficient. This is particularly true if the day is hot and the stone dry (but even new brick adheres better if wet when laid).

After the mortar has been dumped into the wheelbarrow, I position it 4 feet behind the working area. I place pairs of concrete blocks on end one-third and two-thirds along the length of the wall, lay 2-foot squares of plywood on top to act as mortar boards, and eliminate a good deal of needless walking and stooping.

I use a trowel with a 10-inch pointed blade to transfer mortar and shape it as needed. All dimensions are approximations and done by eye.

Erecting the Stone Exterior Wall

I deposit a bed of mortar at the corner 1 1/2 inches thick, 4 inches wide and 4 feet long. As pictured, I lay the first stone so that its end lies in the same

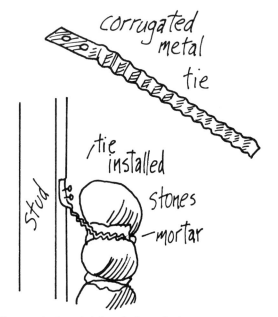

Corrugated metal tie; tie installed

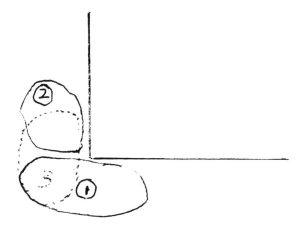

plane as the intersecting wall and ¹/₂ inch away from the sheathing. I tap the stone down gently and decrease the mortar bed to ³/₄ inch. (I will be maintaining a ³/₄-inch-thick bed of mortar whenever possible.) I lay the second stone on the intersecting footing so that its end lies in the same plane as the first. I scrape away excess mortar, fill the gaps around the stones with it, and return what is left to the wheelbarrow. I deposit a bed of mortar 1 ¹/₂ inches thick on top of the two stones, note the contour of the gap between the stones, and lay the third stone so that it best fits the contour. I tap it down gently and decrease the bed to ³/₄ inch. One end of the third stone, as pictured, lies in the same plane as the two stones below it.

I position a small piece of scrap 1-inch pipe on the footing beside the first stone. In about half an hour, after I have laid stones around and above the pipe and the mortar has stiffened sufficiently, I slide the pipe out and the remaining hole provides an exit for water that accumulates on the back side of the stone wall. (I provide weep holes in the same manner every 3 feet.)

The stones, of course, are different sizes and shapes. Uniformity cannot be achieved—nor is it particularly desirable—but if variations are to be kept to a minimum, stone diameters should be held within 5 to 7 inches and smaller or larger sizes discarded. Personally, I prefer the wall to have an exaggerated three-dimensional appearance and place smaller and larger stones adjacent to one another. Whether the irregularity is to be minimized or accented, the wall still has to be plumb; this is achieved by maintaining the ¹/₂-inch gap between the sheathing and the back of the stone. On the exposed side, stones large enough to extend more than 4 inches beyond the median should not be used.

If one feels apprehensive about maintaining the ¹/₂-inch gap by eye, a scrap of ¹/₂-inch material should be placed against the sheathing, the stone being laid butted to it, and the scrap removed.

The first course of stone is laid in the manner previously described along the entire length of the wall. No cutting of stone is necessary since the final gap can be closed with a smaller or larger stone as needed or by increasing or decreasing the thickness of the mortar joints. (In this installation, stone-cutting is eliminated completely.)

From time to time as the first course is being laid, mortar is squeezed out at the back and rests against the sheathing (that is against the tar paper stapled to the sheathing). Unless the buildup of mortar becomes sizable enough to block water from draining, it need not be removed and its presence further helps to stabilize the wall.

After I have completed the first course, I return to the original corner and remove excess mortar around each stone. The amount to remove is primarily an aesthetic choice. From a structural consideration, no more than a third of the stone should be exposed without mortar surrounding it. I remove excess mortar from all stones.

I continue the first course along the intersecting footing by laying a few additional stones and begin the second course from the stone previously laid at the corner. I overlap a single stone at the corner as a reference for the third course. Starting from the cornerstone of the second course, I complete the second course of stones on top of the first. I lay each stone so that it best conforms to the contour of the gap between the stones below it. This reduces the size of the mortar joint and also saves a good deal of mortar. I maintain at least ³/₄-inch thickness of mortar throughout.

Successive courses are laid in the same manner until the wall reaches a height of 3 feet or so. At this point I install corrugated ties 8 inches from each corner and at 4-foot intervals in the remainder of the wall. (I will also install ties at 5 feet and under the uppermost course.)

When the wall reaches the side trim of the windows, I butt stones against the wood and fill in the rest of the course. Here again, I avoid cutting stone by using smaller or larger ones as needed or by increasing or decreasing the mortar joint.

I continue building the walls until they lie barely above the tops of the windows. I lay a 3-by-3-by-¹/₄-inch angle iron (lintel) across the opening above the window so that the ends of the lintel rest on the wall and *not* the head casing. The back of the lintel rests against the sheathing. I continue the course by laying stone directly on the lintel.

Since the lintel is steel, it will rust and discolor the surrounding area. To prevent this, I coat the steel with resin and hardener plastic or a similar rust preventative. An alternate and superior method of preventing rust is to wrap the lintel in wire lath before installation and cover it with mortar. This requires two coats, each ³/₈ inch thick. The mortar is pressed gently into the mesh during the first coat to obtain a ³/₈-inch thickness and the surface scratched to leave indentations. After allowing a

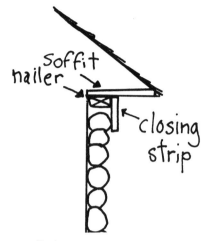

Nailer on soffit for closing strip

day for drying, the first coat is dampened with water and the second applied and finished with a steel trowel.

I pop a chalk line on the soffit that lies just beyond the plane of the wall and nail 2-×-4 cleats along it as pictured. I continue the stone walls to the soffit, fill the joint with mortar, and nail a closing strip to the cleats so that its lower side partially covers the last course of stone.

I apply a bead of silicone caulking in the joints made between the trim of the windows and the adjacent stones and mortar.

I complete the remaining walls in the same manner and reinstall the siding previously removed from the gable end of the house.

The stone facade is the simplest and easiest to erect of all masonry walls. It requires much less time to build than brick or similar materials, provides a distincitive permanent wall that never needs maintenance and will justify its selection as an optimum choice.

PREPARING THE INTERIOR FOR FINISHING

4

Doorway

After the addition has been closed in, providing access to it from the house is continued. The work was begun by denailing and temporarily tacking the sheet or sheets of sheathing in the area the doorway will occupy. The sheathing should now be removed.

Even if there isn't an outlet in the doorway area, a cable bringing electricity to a nearby one will probably be exposed since the usual procedure is to run them in the walls. (Cables may also be strung under the floor and up to the outlet or in the attic and down to it.) To remove the cable from the doorway-to-be, I must first shut off the power in it. (All electrical terms and procedures are explained in detail in the electrical section further on in the chapter.) I place the leads of a test lamp (a light bulb in an insulated sheath with two wires attached) into the slots of the nearest outlet to which the cable is going while a helper goes to the main and begins to switch off breakers. When the light bulb goes out, I call to the helper and the breaker that controls the flow of electricity in the cable is left in the off position. I remove the cover plate of the outlet and remove two machine screws behind

it that hold the receptacle in the box. I pull out the outlet and detach the wires tightened to its terminals. At the point where the cable enters the box, I remove the locknut of the connector and remove the staples holding the cable to wooden members of the skeletal wall. The cable is now free and I pull it out to a point beyond the doorway area. Still working from the addition side, I bore a $3/4$-inch hole outside the doorway area through the shoe and 1 inch in from the edge of the house side. I bore a second hole in the same relative position directly under the outlet box. I thread the end of the cable through the first hole and pull it toward the second hole as far as it will go. Most likely, it will not be long enough to reach the box and I will have to splice an additional length of cable. Since code and safety require that splices be contained within a box, I obtain a junction box for this purpose. I mount the box on any secure wooden member, remove the appropriate knockout, and secure the cable with a connector so that about 8 inches extends beyond the box. I thread a second length of cable through the hole and into the outlet box and secure it with a connector so that 8 inches or so extends from the box. I run the opposite end into the junction box, secure it with a connector, and leave 8 inches extending out of it. I strip ⁵/₈ inch of insulation from the white and black wires contained in the cables and join white to white and black to black wires by screwing a wire nut over the exposed ends. I join the two bare copper wires together with a wire nut. In the outlet box, I strip insulation from the ends of the wires and attach the white wire to the silver-colored terminal and the black wire to the brass-colored terminal on the opposite side of the receptacle. I attach the bare copper wire to the box with a ground clip and reattach the small bare wire from the green hex screw of the receptacle to the box with an additional ground clip. I staple the cable to a stud within 12 inches of the box and at 4-foot intervals. I reattach the receptacle to the box with the two machine screws, attach the cover plate with a single screw, and rerouting the cable is finished.

A 30-inch door is sufficiently wide for normal use but may be wider or narrower in 2-inch multiples from 24 to 36 inches (standard sizes.) To install a 30-inch door, a r.o. for it will have to be provided and I begin by removing the baseboard and ceiling trim from the house side of the common wall. I now want to remove the wall covering that lies in the doorway-to-be area. If the covering is made of individual boards, I place a scrap of 2 × 4 on a vertical joint and hammer along its length from the addition side until the board is loose enough to pry away. After one board is removed, the others come away easily by prying at nail locations with a flat bar. I remove as many boards as necessary to obtain an opening that is at least 32 inches wide.

If the wall material is sheetrock, I pop parallel chalk lines 32 inches apart and cut along the lines with a keyhole saw from floor to ceiling.

Using a cat's paw, I remove all nails from the ends of studs that lie within the r.o. and hammer their tops and bottoms forward so that only 1 inch or so remains on the shoe and under the plate.

I mark the 32-inch width of the r.o. on the shoe and plate, nail a jack and stud together for each side, and install them. I make up a header composed of two 2 × 4s, 35 inches long, with a strip of ¹/₂-inch plywood and glue sandwiched between them. I place the header on edge with its ends resting on the jacks and nail. I cut a 2 × 4 to fit between the top of the header and plate and

position it approximately without nailing in the center of the opening. I tap all members forward until the previously denailed studs are knocked out and the new assembly positioned in the opening. I nail studs to the shoe and plate and shift and nail the 2 × 4 above the header to retain the 16-inch module. I remove the portion of the shoe that lies in the r.o. by handsawing. I cut and reinstall the wall covering around the r.o. After the wall covering of the addition has been applied, I will complete the r.o. with a frame, door, and trim.

Placement of the Tub

Bathtubs are manufactured in steel or cast iron. Although steel tubs are much cheaper, they should be avoided since their porcelain skin chips and discolors easily and does not provide durable service. The type I have chosen is cast iron that measures 32 inches wide, 16 inches high, and 60 inches long and has only one 60-inch side finished. The remaining three sides butt skeletal walls and their edges are covered by material applied to the walls. The tub is ordinarily placed on a plywood subfloor, but since I intend installing a masonry floor over the slab and allow 4 inches for its thickness, I want to elevate the tub slightly less than that distance to avoid the needless difficulty of getting in and out of a tub that has an excessive variation between the floor and bottom of the tub. I therefore assemble a frame of 2 × 4s on edge that measures 52 inches long and 32 inches wide with 2 × 4s spaced 16 inches apart along the length. I position the frame on the slab where the tub will be located and secure it by nailing to the adjacent walls and slab, leaving an 8-inch-long area clear at the drain end.

With two helpers, I bring the tub into the bathroom through the opening left by omitted studs and place it on top of the frame. I check the level of the tub and, if necessary, shim it to a level position. The interior of the tub is sloped down to the drain and unless the tub is level, water will not leave it properly, if at all.

Along the 5-foot unfinished side of the tub, I pop a level chalk line that corresponds to the underside of the tub's edge and nail a 2-×-4 cleat on edge to the adjacent studs. I shift the tub so that its unfinished 60-inch side rests on the cleat and the drain end butts the common wall studs. I install the omitted studs in the wall at the opposite end of the drain so that their 1 1/2-inch sides butt the tub. To provide a nailing surface for later use, I nail cats between studs around the perimeter of the tub so that their lower edges are flush with the top of the tub.

The pictured fittings should be supplied with the tub at the time of purchase. They are typical of all tubs and differ only slightly among different manufacturers. (All manufacturers supply adequate instructions for assembly.)

The drain hole in the tub has a circular indentation around it and I lay a circle of 1/4-inch-thick plumber's putty in it. I position the waste and overflow assembly so that the lower end extends from the drain hole and its upper end at the overflow hole. I secure the assembly to the tub by tightening (each end is threaded) the cover of the pop-up valve and its lever-operated overflow cap. I attach a 1 1/2-by-1 1/2-inch S trap to the drain pipe at the tee with a washer and nut (part of the trap). From the outlet of the trap, I continue with 1 1/2-inch pipe to the previously installed 1 1/2-inch drain that empties into the toilet-bowl drain.

The bowl vent was left with an outlet facing upward. To complete the vent that will serve all three fixtures, I cut a length of 3-inch DWV pipe so that it will extend a few inches above the ceiling. I attach a 45-degree ell to one end and the other end to the fitting outlet. I cannot continue in a straight line since the rafter lies partially in the path of the pipe. I cut a 3-inch nipple, attach a second 45-degree ell to an end, and attach the other end to the first 45-degree ell as pictured.

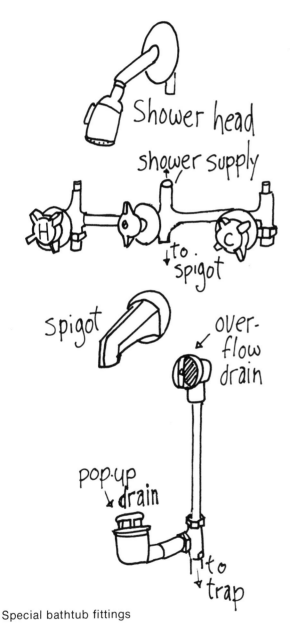

Special bathtub fittings

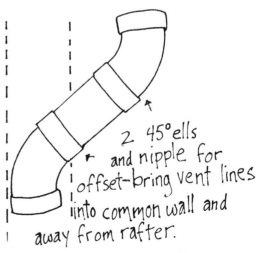

Two forty-five ells and nipple for offset

This offsets the pipe to clear the rafter. Using a string held against the bottom of the roof deck and a plumb bob at the other end, I shift the string until the plumb bob is centered on the upper ell. I mark the spot on the roof deck and bore a pilot hole to the roof. From the roof, using the pilot hole as a center guide, I cut a circle 3 3/4 inches in diameter with a sabre saw. I measure the distance between the top of the roof and shoulder of the ell and cut 3-inch pipe 1 foot longer than the measurement. I slip the pipe down through the hole in the roof and attach the lower end to the ell. To seal the hole between the pipe and roof, I obtain a sheet-metal part called a jack that has an opening made to fit the exterior dimension of the pipe and is sloped to conform to the 4 inch-per-foot pitch of the roof.

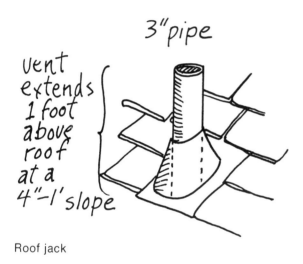

Roof jack

I slide the jack over the pipe, spread plastic tar on the roof in the area the jack will occupy, and lower the jack onto the tar and roofing. I raise the shingles on the high side and lay them over the jack. This completes the roughing in of the drainage system.

Hot and Cold Water Supply

Plastic or copper pipe and fittings are both excellent materials for water lines. Ordinary plastic pipe softens when hot and CPVC, a polyvinyl chloride with an additional chlorine atom, is manufactured to resist heat deformation. It will soften only slightly at 180 degrees and 135 to 155 degrees is the normal hot water temperature in residences. CPVC pipe will also withstand three times the normal 35 pounds of pressure in water lines. Like DWV plastic pipe, both PVC for cold water lines and CPVC for hot are solvent-welded and cut to length with a tubing cutter. Plastic is a good insulator that minimizes heat loss in hot water lines and eliminates sweating in cold water lines. Required fittings are readily available in all plumbing supply houses (cheapest), including special adapters for use in going from metal to plastic. Threaded plastic fittings employ plastic dope rather than ordinary dope used with metal. The plastic-pipe water system has been in use for many years with proven reliability. For the above reasons, and because it is slightly easier to cut and assemble, my first choice for water lines is plastic. However, backward codes in many areas still prohibit its use, so I will detail the universally accepted copper installation. (The procedures are almost identical; if plastic is permitted in your area, I would certainly choose it.)

Copper pipe is manufactured in hard- and soft-temper. Hard-temper is straight and rigid; soft-temper is flexible. Soft-temper is best used in long runs with multiple changes in direction since the pipe can be shaped manually to eliminate fittings. Its flexibility becomes a liability in short runs. I am assuming that the distance between the existing water lines and the bathroom is under 20 feet and will use hard-temper pipe throughout.

Hard-temper pipe is manufactured in three wall thicknesses; the kind best suited for the addition is Type L. Standard lengths are 20 feet. Copper pipe will not rust nor will scale build up inside it. The installation is permanent and trouble-free.

Roughing In Hot and Cold Water Lines

If your existing plumbing is more than 30 years old, the water-supply pipes are most likely galvanized steel. They should be 3/4 inch in diameter but are often only 1/2 inch. (All pipe measurements refer to the inside diameter.)

In the work that follows, existing water lines will be tapped to supply the bathroom. Appropriate valves will be installed close to the taps, one to shut off water to the addition without affecting the rest of the house and another to permit draining the water from the pipes to the addition and prevent freezing and bursting them if the house is left unheated. From the shut-off valves pipes will be run to the addition through the common wall, since it is closest and most accesible and also an interior wall for additional protection against freezing. Each of the pipes will end at the fixtures with a capped nipple that extends beyond the plane of the finished wall. An additional foot of capped pipe will extend upward from both the hot and cold water lines to eliminate water hammer. The nipples emerging from the wall at the basin will be located a couple of inches above the drain and a couple of inches on each side of its center. The nipple extending from the wall to supply the toilet tank will be located 6 inches above the finished floor and 8 inches to the left side of the bowl drain. The hot and cold water lines to the tub will be connected to a special fitting located 8 inches above the top of the tub and recessed 1 1/4 inches in the wall. The valves to control the water supply will be attached to the special fitting and protrude beyond the plane of the finished wall.

Pipes should not be left unsupported for distances longer than 12 feet and the pictured brackets or hangers are used to accomplish this. The hanger has sharpened points that take the place of nails

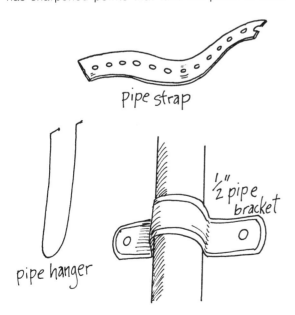

pipe strap

pipe hanger

1/2" pipe bracket

and is used when the pipe is away from a structural member. Brackets are used if the pipe lies adjacent to a structural member. Both brackets and hangers should also be copper; the use of steel against copper leads to corrosion from electrolysis. All pipes should also be supported at the point where they make a turn to emerge from the wall and 1/2-inch pipe clips are optimum in these locations.

When roughing in has been completed and all ends capped, the shut-off valves will be opened and the entire assembly inspected for leaks. If repairs are necessary, they will be made at this time, while joints are accessible and walls not yet closed.

Slip-coupling tee for tapping galvanized lines

The pictured slip-coupling tee will be used for tapping existing galvanized hot and cold water pipes. If the pipes are 3/4-inch, the coupling should be 3/4 by 3/4 by 1/2-inch (1/2 inch refers to the side outlet). If the existing pipes are 1/2-inch, the tee should be 1/2 by 1/2 by 1/2 inch.

I select an area of existing water lines closest to the addition and mark two parallel lines around each that are spaced 1 inch less than the length of the tee. I shut the house valves that control the flow of water in the pipes and place buckets under the portions of pipe I intend to remove. I cut out the marked sections of pipe with a pipe cutter if practical or with a sabre saw and metal cutting blade. I install the slip-coupling tee with its side outlet facing the addition. No threading is necessary and only tightening the nuts and washers inside them at each end is required. The unused remaining outlet is 1/2-inch. All pipes from this point will be 1/2-inch copper and reference to size will be omitted.

Pictured are three types of fittings that will be used often during the installation. They are sweat types made for soldering and each has a shoulder

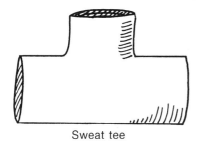

Sweat tee

Ell

Male fitting for solder to thread

that limits penetration of the pipe to $\frac{1}{2}$ inch, the optimum depth.

I cut a 4-inch length of pipe, place it in a vise, and solder a male fitting to one end and a tee to the other. I wrap one turn of Teflon tape around the threads and attach the male end to the coupling, positioning the tee so that the side outlet faces down. I cut another 4-inch length of pipe and attach a water-supply valve with a male outlet threaded to receive garden hose at one end and solder the other end to the side outlet of the tee. I cut a second 4-inch length, solder a shut-off valve to one end, and solder the other end to the remaining outlet of the tee. The first valve will be used to drain the pipes and the second to shut off the water supply to the bathroom. I duplicate the assembly and install it on the hot water line. I close the four valves and reopen the two house valves.

During soldering, there are times when the flame will strike wood; to avoid this danger, I place a piece of asbestos cloth over the wood. There may also be times when heating the fitting will loosen the solder already applied at the opposite end of the fitting, and to prevent this from happening, I wrap the previously soldered joint with a wet rag.

If the existing lines are copper, the pictured saddle tee is preferable to the slip-coupling for tapping. The tee is simply clamped over the existing pipe and a drill bit used to make an opening in

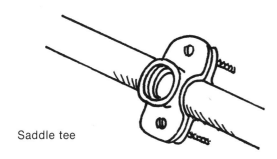

Saddle tee

the pipe that conforms to the shape of the tee outlet. The assembly previously described is now attached to the saddle tee outlet.

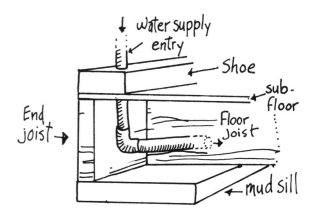

I now want to run the pipes from the shut-off valves to their proper locations in the bathroom. Pictured is a detail of standard construction in houses with basements or crawl space. A mud sill is attached to the top of the foundation wall, a joist laid on end around the perimeter, a plywood subfloor nailed to the joist, and a 2-×-4 shoe laid flat on top of the plywood. Since only 1 $\frac{1}{2}$ inches of the joist lies under the shoe, the remaining 2 inches of the shoe is clear underneath for a depth of 8 inches or so and provides an optimum location to bring in the water lines.

Using the center of the basin drain as a reference, I bore two $\frac{3}{4}$-inch holes through the shoe and subfloor. The center of the hole lies 1 inch in from the shoe on the house side and 2 inches on either side of the drain. The holes are slightly larger than needed for easier alignment of pipes.

Since I want the pipes to drain, I will pitch them upward from the shut-off valve a minimum of $\frac{1}{4}$ inch to the foot. I measure the sloped distance between the cold water shut-off valve and hole, cut a length of pipe 1 inch longer than the measurement to allow for pipe entry into fittings at each end. (Allowance for pipe entry into fittings is made throughout and I will omit further reference to it.) I solder an ell to one end and solder the opposite end to the shut-off valve so that the outlet of the ell faces upward directly under the hole in the shoe. I secure the pipe with clips or hangers.

I measure the distance from the ell to a point 6 inches above the projected finished floor height of the bathroom and cut a length of pipe 1 inch longer. I solder a tee to one end, slip the other end down through the hole, and solder it to the ell with the side outlet of the tee facing the bowl.

I cut a length of pipe to reach 16 inches above finished floor height from the vertical outlet of the tee, install a second tee at one end, and solder the other end to the first tee so that the side outlet faces the bathroom. I solder a cap to one end of a 6-inch nipple (length of pipe less than 12 inches) and solder the other end to the side outlet of the tee. I solder a cap to one end of a 12-inch nipple and the other end to the vertical outlet of the tee.

The capped nipple from the side outlet is located on the right side of the drain and will supply cold water to the basin. The 12-inch capped nipple from the vertical outlet prevents water hammer.

I use the same procedure to bring the hot water line from the shut-off valve to the left side of basin drain. To prevent both contact between the hot and cold water lines and installation difficulty, I place the lower tee at 8 inches from the finished floor rather than the 6 inches used for the cold water line.

Pictured is what the installation looks like at this point.

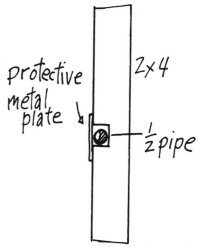

Water pipes recessed in notches in studs

From the side outlet of the tee at the basin located 6 inches above the finished floor height, I want to continue the cold water line to the toilet. Using the center of the bowl drain as a reference, I place a mark on the wall 8 inches to its left, measure the distance from the side outlet of the tee, and cut pipe to length. I attach a tee at one end and solder the other end to the side outlet of the tee at the basin with the side of the tee at the bowl facing the bathroom. I solder a cap to the end of a 6-inch nipple and solder the other end to the side outlet of the tee at the bowl.

To keep the pipes from projecting beyond the plane of the wall, I recess them in notches as pictured. Notches are made by setting the portable

Rough plumbing at basin

saw blade to cut at a depth of 1 inch, scoring the edge of each stud with two passes and knocking out the piece of wood between them with a hammer. After pipes are laid in notches, I nail a protective strip of metal over the face of the notch to prevent nails from puncturing the pipes.

At this point I have a side outlet of a tee at the basin still unused to supply hot water to the tub and a side outlet at the toilet to provide cold water.

I nail a cleat between the studs on each side of the drain end of the tub that is located 8 inches on center above the top of the tub. It is recessed 1 1/4 inches in from the edge of the studs and provides a surface to attach the inner portion of the faucet assembly pictured earlier. In a similar position 7 feet above the finished floor, I nail a second cleat to secure the shower pipe and fitting to be installed. Using the tub drain as a center reference, I mount the rear portion of the faucet assembly on the lower cleat so that its center corresponds to the center of the drain and lies 8 inches above the top of the tub.

I continue the cold water line from the side outlet at the bowl and connect it to the inlet on the right side of the mounted fitting (the necessary nut for attachment is part of the faucet assembly). I continue the hot water line from the side outlet of the tee at the basin and connect it to the left inlet.

I measure the distance from the upper outlet of the center valve to the 7-foot mark on the cleat, cut pipe to length, solder a male fitting to one end, and attach the lower end to the upper outlet of the mounted faucet assembly. I wrap one turn of Teflon tape around the threads of the male fitting at the upper end and screw a 1/2-inch ell to it so that the opening faces the bathroom. I cap a 4-inch threaded nipple and tighten the other end into the ell. (I will remove the nipple later and substitute the shower nipple and head.)

At the bottom and center of the mounted fitting is an outlet and fitting to attach the water supply to the spigot. I cut a 6-inch nipple (some manufacturers supply this assembly), solder an ell to one end, and attach the other end to the mounted fitting. I measure the distance between the shoulder of the ell and the projected plane of the finished wall. I cut pipe to that length, solder a male fitting to one end, and attach the other end to the ell. This leaves the threaded part of the fitting extending beyond the plane of the wall. I screw a cap onto the threaded end.

Three threaded openings in the mounted fitting face the bathroom. I thread the hot water valve into the opening on the left side and the cold water valve into the right. The middle valve, used to divert water from the spigot or shower, is screwed into the center opening. (The threads are especially machined so that no dope or tape is required for a seal.) I attach the handles of the valves temporarily and shut them. (I will remove the handles after testing for leaks and cover the valves with protective cardboard cylinders supplied by the manufacturer while finishing the installation.)

To test for leaks, I first make sure that all pipe ends are capped and open both shut-off valves near the taps. Large leaks are immediately apparent, but fifteen minutes or so should be allowed for pin leaks to develop.

If a leak is evidenced, I shut the valves and attach a garden hose to the cold water drain valve and place its end at any convenient draining spot that is lower than the valve. I open the valve, permit the water to drain, and do the same at the hot water drain valve. (Soldering cannot be done with water in the pipes.)

To repair the leak, I heat and disassemble the joint, wipe off excess solder, clean the pipe end and fitting with emery cloth, resolder, and retest.

This completes roughing in the plumbing. In the final stage that will begin after the walls and floor of the bathroom have been completed, I will install the basin, toilet tank and bowl, and the remaining fittings for the tub.

Electrical Work

Electrical work, like plumbing work, is done in two stages: roughing in and finishing. Pictured are four materials used during roughing in. Staples, a fifth material, have sharpened ends and are driven like nails to secure cable.

The pictured Romex is flexible, nonmetalic, sheathed cable designated #12, 2-wire with ground, the type that will be used exclusively. The cable contains three wires under an outer sheath of insulation. One wire is covered with black insulation and will be conducting 120 volts. (In actual practice voltages vary between 110 and 120 and the utility normally maintains the voltage within 10 percent of these limits.) A second wire is covered

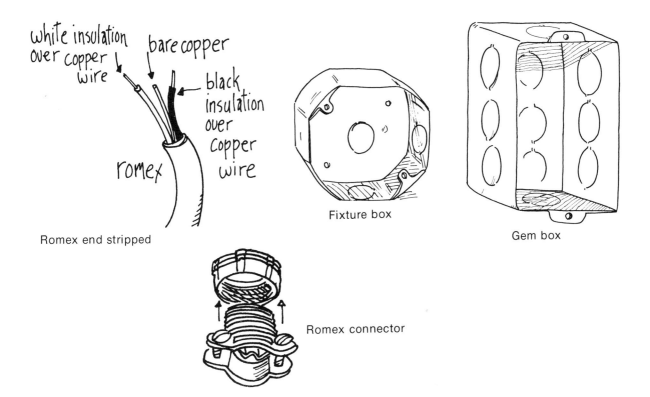

white insulation over copper wire

bare copper

black insulation over copper wire

romex

Romex end stripped

Fixture box

Gem box

Romex connector

with white insulation and will be used to conduct spent electricity into the ground. The third wire is bare copper and will be used to conduct stray electricity into the ground. The cable will be secured to stationary members of the structure with staples and with connectors at boxes. Cable may be strung through holes bored in wall studs, under or through joists, in the attic or basement.

The rectangular metal box, commonly known as a gem box, is required by electrical codes for housing outlets, switches, and wire ends. It is slightly under 2 inches wide, 3 inches high, and 2 1/2 inches deep. Two built-in connectors at the top and bottom of the rear are used to secure incoming and outgoing cable. A single machine screw loosens a clamp to permit positioning of the cable and tightens the clamp over the cable. The box is secured to studs with two #10 common nails inserted into matched predrilled holes in each side of the box. The pictured gem box is the cheapest of many varieties and performs its functions satisfactorily.

Circular indentations in the box called knockouts are easily removed by tapping with a screwdriver till loose and bent back and forth with pliers. The resulting hole permits entry or exit of cable.

The front of the box has two small semicircular projections centered at top and bottom called ears.

Each ear has a small threaded hole used to attach outlets or switches to the box with machine screws.

The sides of the box are secured with a machine screw and bent tab that may be removed so that two boxes can be joined by removing adjacent sides and connecting the two boxes with the same screws and tabs.

The hexagonal box, commonly known as a fixture box, is used wherever a light fixture is to be installed. Some fixture boxes have an attached bracket for mounting with nails; they may also be obtained with a sliding bracket for exact positioning between joists or studs. They may also be mounted to a previously installed cleat and secured with wood screws through holes in the back. The fixture box also has ears with threaded holes that are spaced to match holes in fixture canopies for attachment of the fixture to the box with machine screws.

The fourth pictured item is a Romex connector, used to secure incoming and outgoing cable from boxes that do not contain built-in connectors. The connector has two parts: a hollow male-threaded piece and a locknut. The threaded piece is slipped over cable and a machine screw on either side turned to lower a clamp to secure the piece to the cable. The threaded piece is then placed in the hole provided by the knockout, the locknut slipped over the end of the cable and tightened to the threads from inside the box to secure the cable.

Codes require that an outlet be installed for every 12 feet of usable wall space. (Doorways, closets, and the like are not considered usable wall space.) Six outlets in the room and an additional one in the bathroom are more than sufficient. I will also be installing a ceiling light in the room and a wall light above the basin in the bathroom, both controlled by wall switches. (The switch and outlet in the bathroom will be contained in a double gem box.)

If one assumes that 100 watts will be used simultaneously at all outlets and lights, the total demand will be 1000 watts. The circuit being installed is rated at 20 amperes, 120 volts and provides a theoretical capacity of 2400 watts. In practice, the 20-ampere breaker controlling the circuit will trip before its theoretical capacity is reached and a maximum of 2000 watts can be expected. This amount is double the projected use and will provide more than enough electricity for normal use without overloading the circuit.

If one intends to install a heavy-duty air conditioner or a similar appliance that uses a good deal of electricity, a second or third circuit can be installed using the exact procedures to be detailed.

Roughing In the Wiring

One should first stand in the addition and visualize the placement of furniture to determine where outlets will be most useful. Mark the locations of outlets on studs 14 inches above the finished floor, a height practice has shown is most convenient. Nail the gem boxes to the studs so that they extend beyond the plane of the studs a distance equal to the thickness of the projected wall-covering material. The wall covering will be cut around the box and should lie in the same plane so that the cover plate of the box will lie flat against the wall. All boxes should be installed similarly and I will omit further mention of this detail.

The door to the addition should swing toward the exterior wall and be hung on the addition side. The switch to control the ceiling light should therefore be placed in the addition on the knob side of the door and at a height of 54 inches from the finished floor. This location is where people, by conventional use, expect the switch to be as they enter the room. I nail the gem box to the stud of the r.o. where it is close to the door but out of the path of the doorway trim to be later installed.

I intend to mount the ceiling light at the center of the room and pop diagonal chalk lines between corners to determine the location. I obtain a fixture box with an attached bracket and nail the box to a ceiling joist.

The door to the bathroom will swing inward and toward the exterior wall. I remove a side from two gem boxes, join them, install a cleat between studs adjacent to the doorway, and mount the double box on the cleat with wood screws through predrilled holes at the back of the boxes. The double box is located just beyond the r.o. and at a height of 54 inches from the finished floor.

I mount a fixture box centered on the basin drain and 7 feet from the finished floor. In this location, the light fixture will not interfere with the operation of the medicine cabinet door and provide optimum lighting with a minimum of glare.

Having mounted all the boxes, I am now ready to run cable from the main.

Romex should be purchased by the roll, 200 feet (even though this is likely to be more than will be needed), since it is much more expensive if purchased by the foot.

The main is often installed in the basement and I assume that it is located there. I want to run a single continuous cable from the main to the double box in the bathroom. (I am assuming that this box is closest to the main.) The path of the cable should make as direct a line as possible and require the least number of holes. If a sill or girder is present (a structural member that supports the floor joists above it and lies at a right angle to them), its side provides a clear partial path that requires no boring of holes. Similarly, if the joists are parallel to the projected path, their sides can be used. If neither condition exists, I bore a series of 3/4-inch holes at midpoint in each joist. To continue the path, I bore a hole through the shoe of the common wall and enter the bathroom. I bore a hole through the plate above the double boxes. I now thread the wire through each of the holes, cross the bathroom above the ceiling joists, continue down through the plate above the boxes, enter the left box of the two (which will later have an outlet), secure the cable to the built-in connector, and leave 8 inches of cable extending from the box. (All cable at all boxes should extend 8 inches for ease in making later connections. I will omit further reference to this detail.)

Within a foot of the box, I secure the cable to a stud with a staple. (All cable will be secured by a staple within 12 inches of each box and I will omit further reference to this.) I secure the cable to studs every 4 feet with additional staples. (Same through-out.) No staples are necessary for cable threaded through holes since the hole itself secures the cable. I return to the main, cut the cable 2 feet longer than necessary to reach the main, and take the remainder of the roll to the bathroom.

I now want to run cable from the box nearest the bathroom door (which will later contain the switch) to the box mounted above the basin. To provide a path for the cable, I bore a hole in the plate above the box and another hole in the plate above the fixture box. I thread wire through the holes and secure the end in the fixture box after running the cable over the ceiling joists. I cut the cable from the roll and install this end in the box closest to the door.

I now want to run cable between the outlet box in the bathroom and the closest box in the room. To provide a path, I bore holes roughly centered in studs. I thread wire from the roll through the holes and secure the end in the closest box. In the bathroom, I cut the cable and install this end in the outlet box. (In both instances I first remove the appropriate knockouts, those that lie in the project-ed path of the cable.)

From the second outlet box (in the addition), I bore holes in roughly the center of studs to provide a path for the cable to the next nearest gem box. I thread cable through the holes from the second box and secure the end of the wire in the third box. I cut the cable from the roll at the second box and install this end in the second box. In exactly the same manner, I run cable into and out of all outlet boxes and then arrive at the switch box beside the doorway. I bore a hole in the plate above the switch box and run cable from the switch box to the fixture box mounted on the ceiling joist. This completes

the roughing in of the wiring. No connection has yet been made at the main and further work is later continued without electricity present in any wire in the addition.

Insulation

A good deal of misinformation about insulation is now being advertised, an inevitable fallout of the energy-conservation drive. The fact is that the amount of energy saved by using expensive rather than cheap insulation is negligible. In addition, the thicknesses of insulation now required by building codes are far more than necessary and, in areas such as under the floor of enclosed crawl space foundations, a needless expense.

The unit of measurement in rating insulation is the R factor and present building codes specify the minimum R factor for each area of the structure. (The higher the number, the greater resistance to heat loss.) Walls and floors must have a minimum R factor of 11, achieved with 3 1/2-inch-thick fiber-glass insulation; roofs must have 19, achieved with 6-inch insulation installed between rafters or ceil-ing joists.

I install 3 1/2-inch fiberglass insulation in the walls by placing it between studs and stapling the paper flaps on each side to the front of the studs. Staples should be used every few inches. The aluminum or paper cover faces the inside of the room.

I may meet the code by laying 6-inch-thick insu-lation between the ceiling joists with the paper or aluminum side down. (Insulation width is manufac-tured for use with frameworks of either 16-inch or 24-inch centers.)

A superior alternative is to install 3 1/2-inch insu-lation between the ceiling joists and also between the rafters. A dead air space is created, a desirable energy-saving feature.

I remove fiberglass from the paper and use it to fill all gaps between the window frame and 2 × 4s of the r.o. The purpose is to prevent drafts and eliminate a source of heat loss. (This simple pre-caution is far more effective in lowering heat loss than using insulation under the entire floor.)

When the distance between studs is less than 14 1/2 inches, the insulation should not be crammed into the narrower area since this squeezes shut the air gaps between in the fiberglass and destroys its effectiveness. The insulation should be cut to size with a sheetrock knife (cutting is done from the back) and the air spaces retained.

When working in a confined space such as the attic, it is advisable to wear a gauze filter mask and a long-sleeved shirt to avoid itching and inhalation of fiberglass fragments.

I strongly advise *against* the use of polyethylene sheets for covering the walls because excessive condensation occurs within the walls and causes severe rotting.

Fiberglass insulation is the cheapest of all types, easy to install and is the optimum choice.

Ceilings

Sheetrock (gypsum sandwiched between paper) is by far the most widely used material for ceilings and is to the interior of a house what asbestos shingles are to the exterior; a cheap and durable product that is not very appetizing to look at. It costs 6 cents per square foot ($1/2$-inch thickness: slightly less if thinner and slightly more if thicker), and is the cheapest building material one can buy. Sheetrock was introduced on a mass scale shortly after World II and immediately received a deluge of negative propaganda from plasterers' unions. Its use was associated with poorly constructed tract homes and one was led to believe that, like all cheap materials, sheetrock would not stand up to normal use. If you wanted a good ceiling, plaster would have to be used. Even today this erroneous view is widely held despite the fact that sheetrock has proved itself for more than thirty years to be as durable as plaster and a great deal cheaper and easier to install. If one wishes a plain white ceiling, sheetrock is the optimum choice.

Standard sheetrock sizes are 4 by 8, by 10, or by 12 feet. Standard thicknesses are $1/4$ inch to $5/8$ inch in $1/8$-inch multiples; $3/8$-inch is adequate if ceiling joists are spaced 16 inches on center but should be $1/2$-inch if they are spaced 2 feet on center to minimize waviness that will develop over the years. Since the addition is 20 by 20 feet, 4-by-10-foot sheets should be used to keep the number of joints to be finished to a minimum.

Sheetrock is cut to size by scoring its front with a

sheetrock knife (a razor blade in a holder) and folded along the scored line. The sheet is then cut through along the crease at the back. Sheetrock is installed to ceiling joists by nails spaced 8 to 10 inches apart. The hammer is driven into the sheetrock to leave an indentation around the nail head without breaking the paper surface and the depression filled at a later time.

The material used to fill the depression and smooth it into the same plane as the sheet is joint compound, a cementatious adhesive material manufactured for this sole purpose. In finishing joints between sheets, joint compound is used in conjunction with a paper product called tape. The long sides of the sheets are tapered for a few inches and form an inverted V after installation that allows for filling and finishing the joint so that it is flush with the surrounding surfaces. The 4-foot sides are not tapered and require a special procedure for finishing, since the existing joint is already flush with the rest of the sheet. Joint compound is a material designed to be applied as a *film* and, except for nail indentations, should never be thicker than $1/8$ inch in any single application or multiple cracks (alligatoring) will occur. Alligatoring is evidence that joint compound has been applied too thickly and its adhesive power severely diminished. A good application of joint compound does not require sanding, although this is easier said than done. I have attempted to teach hundreds of people to apply joint compound (and will detail the procedure later), but developing a knack is necessary and few students succeeded in making joints that did not require sanding.

After the joint compound has been applied, shellac thinned with 10 percent alcohol, or size, is used to coat the compound and seal it so that it will not bleed or show through the paint. Paint is then applied and, despite advertising assertions, one can expect to use at least two coats and often three to obtain a uniformly white ceiling.

In my opinion, paint is a parasitic product that has outlived its usefulness except for limited decorative ends. It is simply a cosmetic—and a poor one at that, since repainting is required every few years. If a white ceiling is desired, an excellent alternative to paint is vinyl wallpaper. Unlike supposedly washable paint, vinyl paper provides a permanent and washable surface that is readily cleaned by simply wiping with a mop. Vinyl paper, unlike paint, will not chip, peel, blister, or chalk, and although its installation is initially more expensive, the difference will be recovered the day the first repainting would otherwise become necessary. In the long run, vinyl paper will prove to be far less expensive than paint.

When paper is used over sheetrock, tape can be eliminated at joints and only compound is needed to fill them. Three separate coats are still required since the compound contracts during drying and leaves a concave surface. After the final coat, however, the concave portion is too shallow to notice. Sizing is necessary since water in the paste used to glue the paper will be absorbed by the compound unless the surface is sealed. If it is not, the paste will dry to a powder, lose its adhesive quality, and paper in the affected areas will develop bubbles.

A plain white ceiling is used so often, many people do not even consider other possibilities.

The drawing shows two of a great many ways to treat the ceiling at a material cost under $25 and a minor amount of additional labor. Each has the advantage of the eliminating the need to finish joints in the sheetrock, leaving only nail indentations to fill. Used in conjunction with vinyl paper, they are permanent, maintenance-free installations and if their appearance is pleasing, no hesitation need be felt in using either. However, the two treatments are presented to show possibilities of dealing with the ceiling and should be regarded as only a point of departure for the design of an attractive and practical ceiling.

The pictured ceiling is made of tongue-and-groove, V-joint boards. The joint prevents attic dust from falling into the room and the V masks irregularities in the seam. At 17 cents per board foot if obtained from a sawmill (or wrecking yard), wood is initially competitive with finished sheetrock and cheaper in the long run. Rough-sawn or planed boards are nailed at right angles to the joists and provide a maintenance-free ceiling that doesn't change appearance except for slight darkening over the years. Unlike sheetrock, there are no seams to develop cracks, discoloration, or disintegration as a result of leaks in the roof. Wooden ceilings require less time to install and once in place, no further work is needed.

Almost any variety of wood or combination of woods is suitable. Nonlocal woods will be far too expensive and the choice will probably be restricted to white pine or fir.

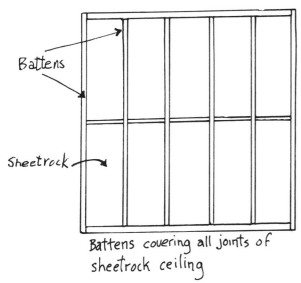

Battens

Sheetrock

Battens covering all joints of sheetrock ceiling

Battens throughout

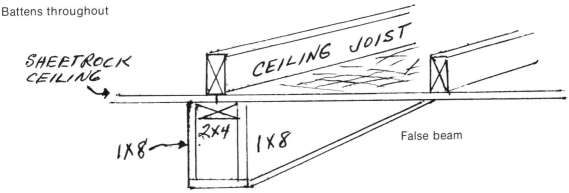

SHEETROCK CEILING

CEILING JOIST

1X8

2X4

1X8

False beam

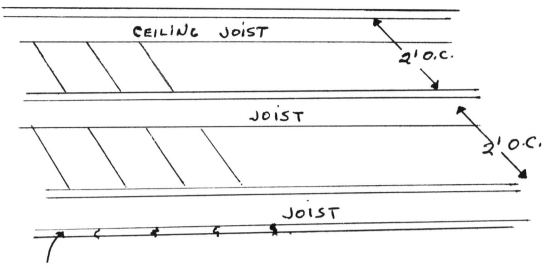

Ceiling paneling nailed to ceiling joists

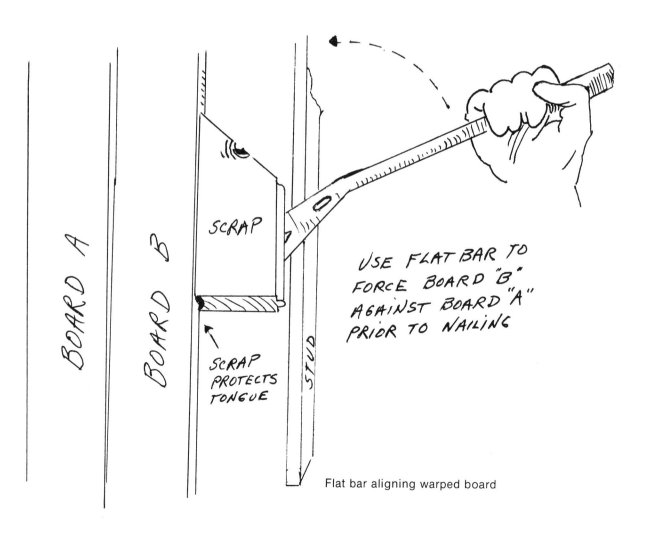

USE FLAT BAR TO FORCE BOARD "B" AGAINST BOARD "A" PRIOR TO NAILING

Flat bar aligning warped board

Gaps between boards are inevitable, but most curves are eliminated in the normal course of toenailing the board to a joist. When the curve is more pronounced, the board is first forced against the previously installed board with a flat bar as pictured. When selecting widths, one should keep in mind that 1 × 4s come together readily, 1 × 6s less easily, and 1 × 8s with difficulty. Wider boards with severe curves are sawed at the curves and installed in two pieces. Toenailing with #6 finishing nails through the tongue side into joists is used throughout except around the perimeter, where facenailing is employed. (The nails will be hidden by the wall covering and optional ceiling trim.)

Treatment of wood is unnecessary for practical reasons but aesthetic considerations may dictate changes. If the natural appearance is to be altered, the wood is first planed. The surface provided by the planer is barely adequate for cosmetic treatment and can be improved vastly by sanding. Even one pass with a belt sander and 120 grit paper makes a marked difference and additional passes with finer paper provide better surfaces for better finishes.

Liming is one of many cosmetic treatments and produces a whitish translucent surface with clearer definition of the grain. A half-and-half mixture of oil-based paint and turpentine is brushed on the board and wiped off with a rag. The longer the mixture is allowed to remain on the wood, the more white the appearance and sharper the definition of the grain. (The grain is denser than its surrounding area and absorbs less material.) One gallon is more than sufficient for the ceiling.

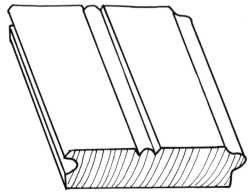

Fir bead and center bead

Fir with bead and center-bead milling was widely used around the turn of the century. It was usually finished with a coat of orange shellac (natural color) followed by two coats of varnish. The resulting color is dark brown with an orange tint; the wild grain is subdued. I lived with this kind of ceiling that, although the finish was done seventy years earlier, was still in excellent condition. Maintenance consisted of running a dry mop over the wood whenever friends remarked about the cobwebs.

Natural oils containing stains and hardeners are available in a comprehensive range of colors and provide an excellent finish that is both durable and easy to maintain. One such product, Watco, is brushed on and wiped off with a rag, dries in a few hours, leaves a tough, hard film over the surface, and is an optimum choice.

Installing Sheetrock Ceiling

Before work is begun, the floor of the addition should be swept and cleared of tools and materials that are not needed. When the sheetrock is delivered, I stack it flat on the floor in the center of the room.

It is advisable to have three people to install 1/2-inch 4-by-10-foot sheets. I've done it alone, using 2 × 4s nailed to form a tee and cleats tacked to plates to support the sheets during nailing, but strongly advise against doing the work alone. Working at a leisurely pace, three people can install the ceiling in two hours or less; if no free labor is available, a couple of people should be hired or the installation will be both laborious and time-consuming.

Sheetrock corners break easily and this usually occurs when someone drops rather than places a corner on the floor. Every broken corner creates an additional twenty minutes of work and often longer to repair.

I place horses and scaffold boards at the intersection of walls No. 2 and No. 3, where I intend to install the first sheet. My head should barely graze the joists when I stand on the boards. Since the addition is less than 20 feet due to the width of the exterior walls, I measure the distance between wall No. 2 and the closest joist to 10 feet and trim a sheet to that length. I tack two 2-×-4 cleats to the plates of both walls in the corner, 3/4 inch or so below the joists in order to hold up the end of the sheet before it is nailed. I lean the sheet against the scaffold boards, the trimmed end positioned to lie against the wall. One person is at the center of the sheet and the other two at the ends. The smooth side of the sheet faces us. We lift the sheet, turn the finished side down, slide the end of the sheet on top of the cleats, butt the edges against the intersecting walls, and maintain the rest of the sheet against the joists with the tops of our heads. Both hands are free, and we drive half a dozen nails through the sheet into the joists. They are sufficient to hold the sheet and take the weight off our heads while nailing is completed.

We move the horses and boards under the intersection of walls No. 3 and the common wall, measure the distance between the common wall and the 4-foot side of the installed sheet, cut a second sheet 1/4 inch less than the distance, and nail it. The trimmed end of the sheet lies at the common wall and the factory end at the joint between both sheets. The 1/4-inch gap enables positioning of the sheet easily and prevents binding during installation. In a similar fashion, we install the remaining sheets.

Each nail is driven below the surface of the sheet and a depression left around the head. One has a reluctance to mar the surface, but without the depression the nailhead cannot be concealed. If a nail is left above the surface, it is usually discovered as a knife and compound are stroked over it. The knife will have to be set aside, a hammer obtained, and the nail driven. This will splatter compound over you and the surrounding area. It is therefore essential to leave the depression at each nailhead during the initial installation.

The sheetrock will have to be cut around the ceiling-fixture box. This can be done before installing the sheet but it is much simpler to nail the full sheet first. I place a scrap of wood over the sheetrock and box and hammer. The outline of the box appears on the surface of the sheet. I cut it out with a keyhole saw and eliminate the need of measuring, marking, and shifting the sheet about to position it properly around the box and seams while the sheet is resting on my head.

Joint Compound and Taping

After the sheets are nailed, the sheetrock is dotted with numerous indentations, joints, and—most likely—some broken corners and gouges.

Shown here are the tools and tape used to convert the surface into a smooth, uniform appearance.

One gallon of joint compound will be needed and

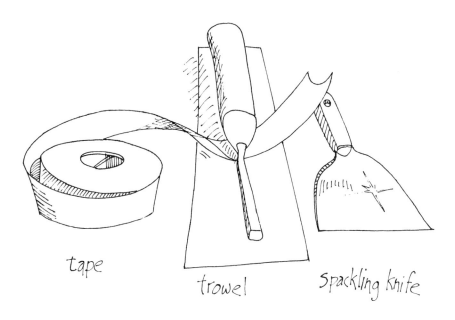

tape

trowel

Spackling knife

can be purchased ready-mixed or in powder form. Powder is mixed with water and is usable twenty minutes later. I much prefer the powder because ready-mixed compound (more expensive) sticks during strokes and leaves an uneven swath, responds far less well to the trowel, and is more difficult to work with in other respects. On more than one occasion these faults were so severe that the ready-mixed compound was unusable. Powder works smoothly and is sold for use in three coats: two gray undercoats are first applied, then a tan finish called topping. Allowing half a pound per sheet, five pounds are needed to finish the ceiling.

Applying First Coat

I mix undercoat powder and water in a clean two-gallon plastic bucket to the consistency of butter at room temperature and allow it to sit for twenty minutes. I cover the bucket with a rag to reduce evaporation and keep foreign material from falling into it. (The compound will remain usable for two or three days if kept covered.)

I arrange horses and boards under a seam so that my head is a foot or so below it. I transfer two fistfuls of compound to the right side of the trowel with the knife. I place compound and trowel against the end of the seam; the long side of the trowel is at a right angle to the seam and open to about a 15-degree angle. With moderate pressure, I maintain the ends of the trowel against the sheetrock beyond the seam and draw the trowel toward me. Excess compound deposited in the joint is removed during the stroke by maintaining the ends of the trowel against the sheetrock and the V depressions between sheets filled. I deposit compound in the V along the entire length of the seam. (The deepest part of the V is only 1/8 inch or so.) The width of the compound is 3 inches or so, sufficient to embed 2-inch-wide tape.

I unroll the tape on the floor from wall to wall and tear it to length. I lay an end against the compound, slide the knife over it to make contact with the compound, and hold up the loose tape with the trowel to prevent it from pulling down the installed portion. I lay the tape against the compound along the entire length of the seam.

I return to the starting point, deposit compound on the trowel, and stroke it over the tape along the entire seam. I open the trowel to a 50-degree angle or so during strokes and use additional pressure to embed the tape a little more deeply and deposit only a slight film over the tape. The additional pressure and steeper angle of the trowel remove any compound that may lie beyond the plane of the sheets.

If portions along the V are not completely filled, I do *not* work on them now but fill them during the second coat. (Once the compound has been deposited and is still wet, further work only makes the area worse.)

If the compound doesn't retain its shape and sags after application, the mix is thin. I add more compound and remix.

If the joint is chewed up due to excessive hammering or mishandling, I remove all loose material from the area, spread a thin film of compound, and allow it to dry overnight. I then deposit additional compound and embed tape as previously described.

If the compound pulls apart or lumps, either it has not been mixed thoroughly or needs additional water.

If any portion of tape lifts after the compound has been applied, I deposit additional compound under and over it and stroke the area with the trowel to remove the excess.

The objective of the first coat is to sandwich the tape between compound adhering to the sheetrock while maintaining the compound at or slightly below the surrounding areas. Even when the compound is flush, it will contract on drying and provide room for successive coats.

After completing the first application, no further work should be done until the compound has dried. Drying is evidenced by a change in color from dark to light gray and will take place in eight hours or so it the room is hot and dry or several days if cold and humid.

Throughout the first application (and subsequent ones), fastidiousness is essential because we are dealing with only a film. Bits of gypsum or hardened particles of compound must be kept from the mix and frequent scraping and discarding compound from the trowel and knife will be necessary. Frequent washing of tools with a sponge is also necessary. If this seems too much of an effort, one should understand that its purpose is to avoid needless sanding, a job that requires a great deal more work.

Compound used to fill depressions around nail heads is thicker than that used for seams because of the relatively small areas involved. I deposit the compound into the depression with the knife at a 30-degree angle and scrape off the excess with a second stroke at a right angle to the first.

Since two strokes only take a second or two, it is tempting to remain at the indentation and fill it fully if this hasn't happened after the first pass. One should avoid the temptation and go on to the next depression since, even when full, the compound will assume a significantly concave shape on drying and the indentation will require two additional passes anyway. Although each pass only takes a couple of seconds, these seconds will be multiplied by the number of nails used and a good deal of needless time and effort will be expended. Three separate applications cannot be avoided to properly fill depressions, so each pass should be limited to two strokes.

Second Application

I mix compound for the second application to the consistency of heavy cream. Holding the trowel at a 45-degree angle, I deposit compound over the seam in strokes as far as my reach. I steepen the trowel angle to 60 degrees and make a second pass over the same area to remove excess compound and smooth what remains in the seam. I repeat the two strokes along the entire length of the seam.

During the second application I fill all hollows left during the first. I also widen the seam to 3 inches wherever needed, simultaneously hiding at least 90 percent of the tape with compound. If I fail to achieve these objectives with two strokes in any area, I do not attempt additional correctional strokes while the compound is still wet and will complete the job on the third application.

If any area of the seam is particularly bad for a foot or more, I remove and discard the compound and apply fresh compound with a heavier-than-usual stroke.

Seams are 20 feet long and, of course, cannot be covered with a single stroke. A trowel mark is likely to remain at the point where successive strokes begin. The only way to avoid leaving the mark is to

develop a "touch" with the trowel and the essential ingredient of this touch is *even pressure on all strokes.* The touch develops with practice and until achieved, the raised lines at overlaps should be left for twenty minutes or so, when the partially dried compound is easier to work. Raised lines are then removed by stroking the knife lightly over them. If one attempts to remove raised lines immediately, additional lines will be created as the initial one is smoothed.

Third Coat

I mix tan topping to a consistency that barely retains its shape but not so loose that it slides off the trowel or water seeps from it.

On the first stroke, I hold the trowel at a shallow 15-degree angle and deposit compound over the seam to fill all depressions left during previous applications and drying. Topping material is composed of smaller particles that pack well, and the contraction during drying is too small to notice. At the shallow angle, compound is also deposited on each side beyond the seam and widens it to 6 to 8 inches. On the second stroke, I turn the trowel almost perpendicular and with moderate-to-heavy pressure remove excess compound and blend the topping into the sheetrock beyond the seam. I apply topping in the same manner along all of the seams and finish filling nail indentations.

I allow the compound to dry, then fill and smooth random spots that have been overlooked. If necessary, I use a vibrating sander and fine emery cloth to smooth surfaces.

Sheetrock is not tapered along its 4-foot sides. Since these joints are already in the same plane as the rest of the sheet, tape and compound over them will be higher than the surrounding area on the first application. In addition, the 4-foot sides are not protected by paper and only slight abuse in handling causes gypsum to fall out. Ordinary nailing along the ends creates a deformed joint that is most difficult to mask satisfactorily.

To treat these seams, I first remove all loose material and renail securely. Compound doesn't "glue" chewed-up material together; any piece that cannot be secured by nailing should be cut out and a new piece substituted.

(Although I am treating the 4-foot joints at this point, in practice I begin them first and work on them intermittently as soon as drying of compound permits.)

I prepare undercoat to a heavier-than-ordinary consistency but not so thick that it pulls apart during strokes. I fill all holes on succesive application, limit the thickness to $1/8$ inch or so, and allow the compound to dry between coats. When holes have been filled to within $1/8$ inch of the surface, I apply compound and tape to cover the seam.

The tape lies $1/8$ inch or so above the plane of the surrounding area. My objective is to create a swath on each side of the tape that will have the shape of a very shallow V. The high point of the V will lie along the center of the V and the low sides will be blended into the sheetrock.

I thin the undercoat to ordinary consistency and deposit it with the trowel on the right side of the seam. I hold one end of the trowel at the center of the seam and the other end against the sheetrock. The angle of the trowel on the first stroke is about 30 degrees. A swath of 6 to 8 inches is deposited. I turn the trowel to almost perpendicular and stroke it over the swath with moderate pressure to remove excess compound and smooth the remainder. I repeat the two strokes on the left side of the seam.

During the final application that is applied in the same manner, I extend the width of each swath to about 10 inches.

The technique is called feathering and, although there is a slight rise from each side to the center, the slope is so small and gradual it cannot be discerned.

Occasionally a bubble will form below the tape due to a lack of contact with the compound. To remove it, I cut the tape out with a sheetrock knife and fill the area as I would a nail indentation.

When one uses joint compound, it is important to understand that the flat ceiling on which it is being applied is a useful tool. The untreated sheetrock areas provide a continuous level reference throughout the process and the trowel or knife must always be making contact with the flat surfaces. An initial tendency to concentrate solely on moving the compound should give way to moving the compound while simultaneously *feeling the flat surface below it along the ends of the tools.* The flat surface permits the trowel to be held with steady pressure throughout a stroke, and steady pressure is essential to avoid waviness and a great deal of needless sanding.

INTERIOR WALLS

5

Practically all material used to cover interior walls is either sheetrock, wood, or masonry, and one has a choice of many products in the latter two categories. Obviously, one's choice should be aesthetically pleasing but if the selected material demands constant attention, its pleasing appearance is bound to fade and with it, an essential element: that the material withstand not only normal use but, preferably, heavy wear and tear. Economy is also an essential element and in this respect, paneling obtained from a lumber yard must be ruled out since its cost is prohibitive but paneling obtained relatively cheaply from a sawmill is an excellent choice. Although this reduces the number of options, there are still many materials left that are aesthetically pleasing, economical, and require little or no maintenance.

If smooth white walls are desired, sheetrock covered with vinyl paper is an optimum choice. Materials cost about 16 cents per square foot and fulfill wall requirements. The sheetrock is installed much as on the ceiling and tape is eliminated in preparation of the surface for paper. The joint between walls and ceiling is closed with tape or hidden by ceiling molding, the joint between walls and floor covered by baseboard or left as is if the use of carpet is projected. Compared to the alternative of plaster and paint, sheetrock and vinyl paper is cheaper by far and much easier to maintain.

If paint is to be used instead of paper, unless one is skilled in applying compound, the objective of a smooth wall should be abandoned or a huge amount of work lies in store. Instead of compound, I would use Tex or a similar product (available in all lumber yards and paint stores). These products leave a slightly textured surface that appears smooth from a few feet away and require no skill to apply. (Adequate directions for use are printed on the container.) They mask seams effectively and are applied quickly and easily.

The cheapest of all woods for interior walls is prefinished plywood. It is commonly marketed in 4-by-8-foot sheets, $1/4$ inch thick, but is also available in other sizes and thicknesses. Sheets are scored vertically to simulate individual boards and the outer ply can be obtained in oak, cypress, pecan, walnut, teak, and a great many other woods. The veneer is factory-treated and has a long-lasting finish that is easy to maintain. Costs begin at about 8 cents per square foot and, since no treatment is necessary after installation, prefinished plywood is the least expensive of all viable wall coverings.

The cost of prefinished plywood rises as better veneers, better glues, and better plies are used. One can expect to pay at least 20 cents per square foot for moderately good quality and a great deal more for fine quality. Above 12 cents per square foot, other products become competitive, and above 16 cents, prefinished plywood is no longer the most economical material that can be obtained from a lumber yard.

White pine paneling is an excellent choice for walls and fulfills all requirements exceptionally well. One can expect to pay 60 cents per board foot and up at a lumber yard, but I paid 17 cents at a local sawmill, a price well within the cost goal of the addition.

White pine is generally light yellow with occasional streaks of tan and a relatively unpronounced grain. Knots are small and tight and occur much less frequently than in other varieties of pine. Although classified as a softwood, white pine is relatively hard compared to redwood or cedar and withstands abuse fairly well. Shrinkage, warping, and checking after installation are negligible factors. I recently visited a home I built twenty years ago, and despite five children in the family, found its white pine paneling in good condition.

Any of the previously mentioned joints is adequate for installation, but tongue-and-groove, V-joint, comes together best. If applied horizontally, boards are simply nailed to studs. If applied vertically, cats are installed at 4 feet to provide a midpoint nailing surface that will maintain the board tightly after it has been aligned. (Additional nailing surfaces are provided by the plate and shoe.) Boards may also be installed diagonally or in designs such as herringbone. Paneling is also used in conjunction with sheetrock by installing it to a 4-foot height (or higher or lower) and the upper part of the wall covered with sheetrock. In addition to aesthetic considerations, in this arrangement the wood provides protection in the lower portion and the overall cost is reduced by using sheetrock for the remainder.

After installation, white pine does not require further treatment unless its natural appearance is to be altered. Left untreated, it will darken slowly and slightly over the years. At 17 cents per square foot, white pine is competitive with sheetrock and

paint or paper and by far a superior alternative.

Hemlock fir obtained from a sawmill at 17 cents is another excellent choice. It is generally tan, with fewer knots than pine, and has a much more pronounced grain. Fir is also harder and tougher than pine and resists damage better, though either wood can be restored easily by sanding. (I've never encountered a situation in which a board was so damaged it could not be salvaged and had to be replaced.)

Fir needs no treatment after installation. If a cosmetic change is desired, Watco with an appropriate stain is simply brushed on and wiped off. Unlike white pine, which is more porous, fir lends itself well to finishing and reveals an extensive and complex grain with high definition.

White pine and hemlock fir are woods widely available locally but the choice is by no means limited to them. In many areas, maple, butternut, cypress, and other woods can be obtained from local sawmills. These woods are prohibitively expensive at a lumber yard but are regarded in local sawmills as just logs to cut and sell at the same price as fir or pine. The amount of wood involved is too little for commercial exploitation and the situation provides the homeowner with an excellent opportunity for obtaining rare and often beautiful paneling at far less cost than pedestrian paneling obtained at a lumber yard.

Shown here is only one of many decorative touches that can be milled at a sawmill for an additional cost of 2 cents per running foot or shaped on the site with a router. Other shapes are displayed at lumber yards, hardware stores, and in catalogues that illustrate the performance of various router bits.

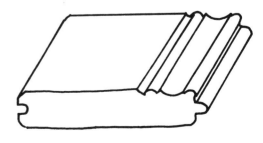

Butterfly pine

Installing 1-×-8 White Pine Paneling Vertically

The techniques and procedures to be detailed are equally applicable to horizontal, diagonal, and other installations and other woods as well.

I pop level chalk lines on the walls at 4 feet and install cats between studs alternately above and below the chalk lines for easier nailing.

I cut all boards ¼ inch less than the distance between the floor and ceiling to allow for variations in height at different points. Each board will butt the ceiling and the resulting gap at the bottom will be hidden by the flooring material or a baseboard.

The first board should be installed on wall No. 1 at the corner with the common wall. Proceeding from left to right around the room, the final board will lie on the common wall and butt the first board. The last board will have to be ripped to remove its excess width that lies within the r.o. The resulting narrower width can more easily be shifted to form a tight joint with the first board along their entire lengths. Since boards are also tongue-and-grooved and only 16 inches of the last board remains at full width, its installation above the doorway is made much easier.

I select a straight board, tack the top to the plate with the board ¼ inch away from the common wall, and plumb it with a level. I facenail the board with two #6 finishing nails ½ inch below the top and spaced 1 ½ inches in from each side. I facenail the bottom 1 inch up from the end, also spaced 1 ½ inches in from each side. I toenail an additional nail through the tongue side into the 2-×-4 cat and drive it below the surface with a nail set. I will use an identical nailing pattern throughout except when otherwise stated.

I split an 8-inch-long scrap of paneling down the middle and keep the grooved piece.

I slip the groove of the second board into the tongue of the first. The fit is sometimes tight and, if necessary, I place the groove of the scrap into the tongue of the second board and hammer the scrap until the second board fits tightly against the first, then nail.

If the board curves outward at the center, I nail the top first and start a toenail at the center. I place the scrap at the curve, insert the tip of the flat bar between the scrap and nearest stud, pry the board

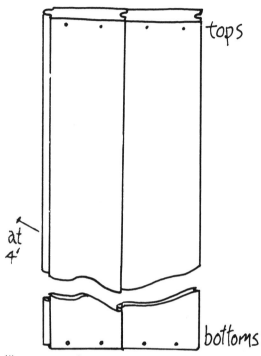

Nailing pattern for paneling

to the one previously installed, and nail. If the curve is severe and the single nail does not hold it, I retighten with the flat bar and toenail an additional nail into the cat. If the board still doesn't hold, I drive a #8 finishing nail through the face—and if this is still not enough, I drive a second nail through the face. If the board still doesn't hold, I remove it and cut it into pieces for use where short lengths are needed.

If there is more than 1 inch between the scrap and stud, leverage cannot be effected and I diminish the distance with a wider scrap or if necessary place a scrap of 2 × 4 against the stud to diminish the distance and make prying with the flat bar effective. My left hand manipulates the flat bar and my right hand is free to nail.

Face nails at midpoint are often necessary to maintain a warped board in alignment. I prefer to leave the nail head exposed. If one wishes to conceal it, the head is driven below the surface with a nail set for an ⅛ inch or so and the hole filled with a pine-colored putty stick.

If the board curves inward at the center, I nail it there first. I position the scrap on the board at the top, drive the V at the end of the flat bar into the edge of the plate, pry the upper end into alignment, and facenail. I repeat this at the bottom.

Spotted about the addition are the previously installed outlet boxes and paneling is cut to expose them completely. I continue the installation until I am less than the width of a board away from a gem box. I stand a board beside the box, butt its end against the ceiling and mark the top and bottom of the box on the board. I measure the distance between the edge of the groove of the installed board and the box and mark the distance on the board. I turn a gem box upside down, align it with the marks, and trace its outline. I cut out the outline with a sabre saw, sawing *on* the lines. The resulting hole is slightly larger than the box and is necessary when tongue-and-groove boards are being fitted. The opening, however, will only be $1/8$ inch or so larger on all sides and the cover plate of the outlet will hide the gaps.

If the box lies entirely within the board, after marking its location, I bore $1/2$-inch holes to expose the ears at top and bottom and use them for entry and cutting with the sabre saw. (A rough-cutting blade at maximum speed works best.)

I continue the installation until I am less than the width of a board from the window frame. I mark the position of the frame on the board as if the frame were a gem box, rip the vertical line with a Skil saw, and cross-cut with the sabre saw. I lay a bead of silicone caulking around the perimeter of the frame to seal the joint between it and the framework and install the board with its back pressed into the caulking. This seals the window frame and effects a saving of energy.

A good practice is to cut pieces above and below the window from the same board, particularly if the window is wider than 4 feet. Boards vary in width and over 6 feet the differences may cause a sizable misalignment of tongues so that when a full board is needed to complete the paneling around the window, tongues will not be in the same vertical plane. (The short pieces that correspond to the height of the window are used above doorways.)

I continue the installation until I am less than the width of a board from the corner. I measure the distance between the edge of the tongue of the installed board and the corner and rip the board $3/8$ inch narrower. This permits the board to be fitted without interference by the intersecting wall and

the resulting gap will be hidden by the board installed next on the intersecting wall.

I continue the installation until I am less than the width of a board from the r.o. for the bathroom doorway. I place a board in the position it will occupy and mark on its back the portion that lies within the r.o. I remove the excess with a Skil saw and nail the board.

I continue the installation until I am less than the width of a board from the first one. I measure the width between the edge of the tongue of the board above the doorway and the corner. I set the blade of the Skil saw at a 45-degree angle and rip the width from the tongueside. (The wider portion of the slant is on the face.) I mark the height of the r.o. on the back of the board and rip the portion of the board lying in the r.o. I slip the remainder of the groove into the tongue of the short piece above the doorway, lay a scrap against it near the top, and hammer forward until the board lies flat against the wall and its right side tight against the first board. I pry the remainder of the board with a flat bar until its right side is tight against the first board also and nail.

If the portion of the last board that lies above the doorway becomes too tight to hammer forward before it is $1\,1/2$ inches from the wall, it's too wide and I trim it with an electric block plane (or manual plane) still maintaining the 45-degree bevel. Ideally, this portion of the board should fit snugly when it is $1/2$ inch from the wall and will form a tight joint with the first board when driven flat against the wall.

An alternative method of fitting the last board is to break off the underside of the groove with a hammer and chisel and lay the board over the gap. The side of the board butting the first board should still be beveled, since it is much easier to make a tight fit along 8 feet if one is dealing with a thin edge rather that its full $3/4$-inch thickness.

General Informattion

During milling of a log, boards of varying widths are first sawed then resawed into uniform widths. This results in a good deal of waste that can be eliminated if random widths are used to panel the room. During installation, additional material is saved since one can select optimum widths whenever ripping is required.

All sawmills deliver square-edged boards, but

some are not able to mill the tongue and groove. Milling can be done at the site with a router and carbide bits to shape the tongue and groove, but this work should not be attempted unless the router is at least 1 1/2 horsepower. Less powerful routers simply won't do the work and their motors are likely to burn out long before the boards have been shaped.

Milling on the site is best accomplished with the router mounted upside down on a router table. (Sears and other national chains sell router tables.) The bit is raised through a hole in the center of the table and adjusted to cut at the required height. The edge of the board is then run along the bit to produce the tongue and the bit changed to produce the groove. Both bits have built-in guides that prevent the wood from being cut too deeply and maintain the required depth. Unless the router is more than 2 1/2 horsepower, milling should be done in several passes rather than a single one and material removed gradually to avoid ripping out chunks of wood, overloading the motor, and dulling the bit prematurely.

If burn marks appear, either the bit is dull and must be reground or the wood is being held too long against the bit and cutting should proceed at a faster pace. If faster cutting results in slowing the router excessively, the board should be eased farther away from the bit, keeping the fast pace but decreasing the amount of wood removed during each pass.

Carbide-tipped router bits are available that not only cut the tongue and groove but simultaneously shape half a V along the edge of the board. The V formed between boards takes the eye away from irregularities in the joint and presents a seeming uniformity that is not actually present. (Bits that will simultaneously cut a butterfly design along with the V are also available.)

The ship-lap joint is adequate but not as satisfactory as the tongue-and-groove joint. In this arrangement a square edge butts a square edge and the fit is generally less tight. Ship-lap joints have the advantage of requiring only a single 3/8-by-3/8-inch rabbeting bit for shaping but one should expect to spend more time to achieve satisfactory alignment between boards.

If only square-edged stock can be obtained from a sawmill and only manual means exist to mill

joints, boards can be facenailed and the sides butted. It is unrealistic to expect good joints and gaps will be clearly visible. A huge amount of work is required to fit boards manually and it is much simpler to hide the joint with a batten. In usual installations, the batten is 2 inches wide and 3/8 inch thick when used with an 8-inch board but, of course, widths can be varied to suit one's taste. Battens are simply nailed over the joints.

A variation of the board-and-batten arrangement is to install the battens first and nail boards over them spaced 1 inch or so apart. For cosmetic reasons, the battens can be treated with darkly stained Watco to provide contrast with the lighter wood or covered with black formica or any other variously colored laminate.

In addition to the 4-foot-high wainscoting previously mentioned, boards can be arranged into 4-foot squares and the same or contrasting woods used to fill the center. The arrangement is particularly valuable when only a limited amount of exotic wood is available and has to be stretched over the entire interior.

Secondhand lumber obtained at wrecking yards is also a good source of wood. Its cost is generally lower than lumber-yard prices and a good deal higher than at sawmills. A common practice on the West Coast is to sandblast the wood. The result is a clean surface striated by higher grain lines that is an attractive wall covering. I would entertain this possibility only if wood cannot be obtained from a sawmill.

Masonry Walls

The interior wall finished with plaster or stucco is still common though in deep decline. Costs, compared to sheetrock, are so high and advantages so slight that both must be ruled out as a viable choice.

All other masonry products suitable for walls are also too expensive if obtained commercially but stone is free or very cheap and a material that makes an excellent interior wall. Almost any kind of stone is suitable, but slate is a particularly happy choice because it is easily shaped into usable pieces and is abundant in a great many areas.

Slate formations occur naturally in layers and where nature has not already separated them through freezes and thaws, layers can be loosened easily by pounding the tip of a flat bar into a seam. (It took me four hours to cut 700 square feet of slate from a single rock using a flat bar and 5-pound hammer.) If an impact chisel is available, the work can be done in less than an hour. Pieces too large to work with are easily broken into smaller ones with a cold chisel and a few blows from a hammer. Layer thicknesses vary and are commonly between $1/2$ inch and 3 inches. All but the thickest can be used for the interior wall.

Slate can be laid flat to expose its thin sides or on edge to present a much greater surface. If laid flat, only pieces 6 inches or smaller should be used or the thickness of the walls will intrude excessively into the living space. A great many more pieces are needed if slate is laid flat, but the installation is much simpler than if laid on edge. Slate laid flat is installed in the same manner as the exterior stone wall previously detailed.

If slate is laid on edge, the number of pieces required is much less but each piece will have to be contoured around its perimeter to correspond to shapes of adjacent pieces. Trimming the perimeter is done by chipping the edges with a brick hammer and performed with a "light" hand since the force required is minimal. A good deal of time can be spent in shaping precisioned parallel contours between pieces, but it can also be done roughly and quickly since the joints between pieces will be filled with mortar.

Mortar used throughout is the same as for the exterior wall: 1 part cream, 2 parts cement, 8 parts sand, and enough water to obtain a consistency of butter at room temperature. The mortar dries to light gray and contrasts sharply with the darker slate. If the joints are relatively wide (more than $3/4$ inch), the contrast will be heightened even further. Personally, I dislike the contrast and prefer to accent the continuously irregular surface of the slate. To diminish the presence of the mortar, I use a type of cement called "black velvet" that contains mineral oxides and dries black. (The color is permanent.)

Another possibility is using white cement in the mortar to emphasize the joint. When this is done, I take additional pains to trim contours better and keep the width of mortar joints less than $3/4$ inch and preferably $1/2$ inch. If the joints are wider, they tend to dominate the appearance of the wall and substantially reduce the impact of the slate.

Slate varies in color and is usually dark gray to blue-black. Erosion leaves dust on the surface and the true color of the slate remains hidden until scrubbed. I have enhanced the color further by rubbing used crankcase oil into the slate. The transformation is like planing a board and revealing its formerly hidden grain. After several rubbings, oil ceases to come off the surface and the finish lasts indefinitely.

In weighing the use of slate, one should keep in mind that, like most masonry materials, it has a massive appearance and dominates a room. If the exclusive use of slate is visualized as too much, I would consider it for one or two walls or for smaller sections between paneling. Slate is simply too fine a building material and too good a buy to dismiss without serious consideration.

Installing Slate on Edge

Slate laid on edge does not form a self-sustaining wall and has to be supported by backing. Backing consists of a $3/4$-inch-thick concrete wall reinforced by lath and applied in two coats, each roughly $3/8$ inch thick.

I staple tar paper over the skeletal wall to act as a vapor barrier, then nail 2-by-8-foot sheets of wire lath (steel mesh with diamond-shaped holes) to the wall. I use straight-cutting Wiss shears to remove pieces of lath that lie over electrical boxes and secure the edges with additional nails. (The cut ends of the lath are sharp and should be folded away from the hand during cutting.) The lath serves as an armature to hold the first coat (scratch) and provides a great deal of additional strength to the wall.

I nail $3/8$-by-2-inch slats along the bottom of the shoe and top of the plate. These pieces are called grounds and are a $3/8$-inch thickness reference during application of the first coat. They also provide a nailing surface for floor and ceiling trim.

I select a straight 1 × 3 and cut it $1 1/2$ inches less than the distance from floor to ceiling. The board is used to flatten applied mortar by stroking it on a slight diagonal (screeding) with its ends resting against the grounds at the top and bottom of the wall. Screeding reduces the thickness of the concrete to ³/₈ inch and reveals shallower areas where additional material is needed.

I prepare a batch of mortar, dump it into a wheelbarrow, and bring it to the wall. I transfer about a tenth of the mix to a 12-inch magnesium square with a carrying handle underneath, a portable mortar board called a hawk.

I place the hawk near the bottom and corner of the wall. Using a 10-inch pointed trowel, I push half a fistful of mortar *gently* against the lath. (Half a fistful is an amount an inexperienced person will have no trouble manipulating.) A light touch is essential or the mortar will simply be pushed through the mesh and fall from the opposite side.

As I deposit the mix on the lath, I note whether it retains its shape and doesn't pull apart, indications of its optimum workability.

If the mix runs or sags of its own weight, I thicken it with additional cream, cement, and sand in a 1-2-8 proportion until it retains its shape.

If the mix pulls apart as I pass the trowel over its surface, I thin it with water until it barely stops pulling apart.

I keep the hawk butted against the lath to partially relieve me of the mortar weight. In this position the hawk is also always closest to the point of work and reduces application strokes necessary to simply slide the mortar from the hawk to the lath.

I continue to apply small amounts of mortar to the lath on each application stroke until I have covered an area from floor to ceiling about 18 inches wide. (If the day is hot and dry, I will only do 1 foot and if cold and wet, 3 feet or so.)

I place the ends of the screed board on edge against the top and bottom grounds and with short strokes on a slight diagonal, pass the screed board over the applied mortar. The objective of screeding at this point is not a "finished" smooth surface but merely a rigid one with a rough surface that is essentially flat and ³/₈ inch thick. It is unnecessary to fill all bare areas but at least 90 percent of the lath should be covered.

I continue across the entire wall in the same manner and leave it undisturbed for a couple of hours. I return with a scrap of lath and scratch horizontal lines into the surface over the entire wall. Supposedly the scratches provide a better surface for the second coat to adhere to, but I

suspect that its continued use is more out of habit than value.

During application and screeding, concrete passes through lath holes and droops along the back of the lath. Blobs larger than lath holes are formed that harden into "keys" and provide structural stability. During the first twenty minutes or so after the concrete has been applied to the lath, bonds that are being established in the concrete are still weak and shifting the material about does not destroy them. As more time elapses, bonds become progressively stronger and shifting concrete at this time destroys its ability to form strong keys. Keys broken before they have had enough time to set will not re-form and shifting the concrete *after twenty minutes* should not be done. (The maximum time will vary and be longer on cold and wet days; twenty minutes is maximum for a hot and dry day.) I wait at least twenty-four hours and preferably forty-eight before resuming work on the wall.

While the scratch coat is drying and hardening, I wash the slate and bring it into the addition in a wheelbarrow. I select the largest and thickest pieces for the bottom course and using the floor to simulate the wall, lay the pieces out, shift them about, and trim each piece to fit adjacent pieces until the entire bottom course is laid out. Each piece is positioned in the location it will occupy on the wall. I continue to lay out the wall on the floor in the same manner until it is entirely laid out and each piece separated to allow for mortar joints.

During the arrangement of pieces, I am guided by my preference for a very rough surface without pronounced changes between adjacent pieces. Because a slate wall is permanent, I also elect to spend additional time making tight fits to keep mortar joints within a maximum of ³/₄ inch.

The perimeters of pieces are usually linear rather than curved, and fitting for the most part consists of marking edges with chalk to define the desired line and chipping away excesses with blows from a brick hammer delivered on a slight diagonal outward from the edge.

The drawing shows two types of fit between pieces of slate. Complex joints can be simplified by chipping irregular portions into a line or retained for greater visual interest by making the necessary cuts with a masonry-cutting blade and Skil saw. If

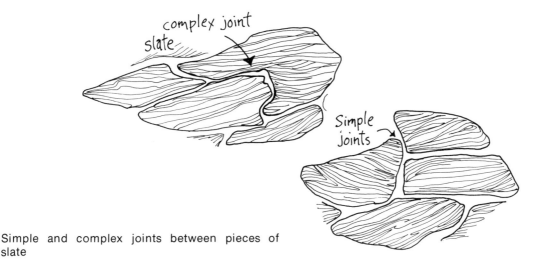

Simple and complex joints between pieces of slate

the thickness of an edge is more than an inch, chipping is easier than sawing. For finer work involving joints of $1/4$ to $3/8$ inch, a heavy-duty carborundum grinding wheel is used after chipping.

I number each piece of slate in the order I will place it on the wall and work from left to right to complete the bottom course. I start the second course at the left, and so forth. I place an arrow pointing upward on each piece and matched lines on adjacent pieces as a reference for identical placement on the wall.

I prepare a batch of mortar with an additional shovelful of cream for increased adhesiveness and pliability. I dampen the scratch coat with a fine spray of water (atomizers for watering plants are good for doing this). Using the hawk and a 16-inch rectangular steel trowel, I deposit mortar on the wall and floor in the corner beside the doorway from the house. I want mortar thickness to be at least an inch. I place the first piece of slate on edge and press it into the mortar until the back of its thickest part lies against the wall. Using the wall as a reference, I tap the edge of the piece as needed to shift it into a plumb position. One's eye is good enough to judge but a plumb bob or level can be used.

I remove excess mortar around the periphery of the piece and use it to fill hollow spots between the back of the piece and the wall. If gaps remain that I cannot reach without removing the piece, I leave the piece if these areas total less than 10 percent.

The problem of noncontact is eliminated if the mortar deposit is a good deal thicker than needed.

I remove mortar around the periphery of the piece where contact will be made with adjacent pieces so that when adjacent pieces are laid, they will make contact with fresh mortar.

I continue in this same manner along the entire bottom course and begin the second course above the first piece laid.

I deposit mortar on top of the first piece's upper edge and on the wall. I lay the slate into the mortar and tap lightly with a brick hammer to align it with the chalk marks.

If the slate sinks of its own weight below the intended position, I thicken the mortar and reinstall the piece. If more than light taps are needed to shift the slate, I thin the mortar.

If the mortar is at the proper consistency and a piece of slate is heavy enough to sink of its own weight below the desired position, I prop it up with wooden shims temporarily, remove the shims after half an hour or so, and fill the holes with mortar.

I remove excess mortar after installing each piece.

I nail corrugated fasteners to every third stud along the third course and place its opposite end on top of second course pieces. I continue the third course over the fasteners. I will also install fasteners at a height of 5 feet or so and under the top course.

I complete the entire wall in the same manner.

A slate wall becomes, from a structural viewpoint,

a single unit after drying. Pieces are maintained in a vertical position mainly by suction, the action of mortar on the back of the slate and on the scratch coat. The weight of the pieces and the ties provides additional strength. (Once the mortar has dried, the force of suction is strong enough to maintain pieces without additional support.)

After a few weeks, I rub used crankcase motor oil into the slate to enhance its natural color and provide a finish that requires no maintenance.

Bathroom Walls

When walls are exposed to a good deal of water and humidity, a suitable covering is particularly desirable. Among many possibilities, water-resistant sheetrock covered by waterproof paper provides the cheapest installation that fulfills (barely) bathroom-wall requirements. Costs begin at 17 cents per square foot and rise as more expensive papers are used.

Water-resistant sheetrock is covered by a water-repellent film and is installed in the same way as ordinary sheetrock. Nail indentations and seams are filled with joint compound and no tape is necessary. Size or shellac is applied over the dried compound and paper hung with vinyl paste rather than wheat for better adhesion. One should expect portions of ends and seams to lift over the years and require repasting, but on the whole the installation is durable and easy to maintain. Suitable papers are available in great variety and can be inspected in home-improvement centers. If the primary objective is the least amount of cost and labor combined with nominal durability and ease of maintenance, sheetrock and paper are the optimum choice.

For a hundred years or so since its introduction from Europe, ceramic tile has been the dominant material for bathroom walls. It is extraordinarily durable (after centuries of exposure, ceramic tiles in the Baths of Caracalla in Rome are still intact) and fulfills all bathroom-wall requirements exceptionally well. The cheapest wall tiles are glazed, nonvitreous 4 1/4-inch squares that retail at 70 cents per square foot; covering the bathroom walls with them would run about $140.

A common practice to reduce costs is to extend the tile to the ceiling in the tub area and only to a height of 5 feet elsewhere. This is a false economy, since the money saved initially will be expended within a few years to maintain the untiled areas. The practice of partially–tiled walls arose when the high labor cost of a tile-setter was required (and masonry walls as backing),but with the introduction of organic adhesives (mastic), an inexperienced person can now install tile more quickly than a professional using masonry methods. Unfortunately, the cost of tile in the United States is enormously and shamefully inflated (tile that is 70 cents here costs 10 cents in Mexico). Despite its high cost, only a relatively small area is to be covered and tile is a viable choice. (Most tile dealers have "remainders"—quantities too small to cover a large area, but adequate for one or more bathroom walls. Prices will be much less than 70 cents.)

Costs are dramatically reduced if tile is purchased at a wrecking yard. The tile will, of course, be secondhand and one should expect to spend time selecting undamaged pieces to obtain a savings of $100 or so. Equally important is the fact that older tiles are almost always much better in quality than newly manufactured ones since wreckers take time to save only the best.

If a decorative tile wall is desired (or if it isn't feasible to assemble 200 square feet of identical used tile), the use of two or more types should be visualized. In this respect, architectural showrooms and interior design magazines regularly display tile arrangements that may prove helpful in creating your own. The practice of installing tile in an institutionally repetitive manner is simply a means of cutting costs in commercial situations and is not applicable to your addition. The most interesting and attractive walls I have built or seen employed tiles of different types, thicknesses, colors, and sizes. Designing a wall of this kind is an opportunity for self-expression that ought not to be passed by. Tiles that are old, varied, beautifully made, and inexpensive are simply too good to dismiss without a serious look beyond mere uniformity.

Stone is also an excellent material for bathroom walls and fulfills all requirements exceptionally well. In addition to slate or basalt, split basalt presents a particularly interesting possibility. Their interiors range in color throughout the spectrum and often have streaks of black or gray ore deposits that provide additional visual interest. The procedure and technique for laying split stone is the same as detailed for exterior walls. (See Index). One should expect a substantial amount of additional labor as compared to other installations since each stone will have to be split, but since the number of stones needed is relatively small and splitting provides two pieces, additional labor is not excessive and is compensated for by the use of a free material that results in a unique and permanent installation. (Stones are split by striking with a pickaxe, a brick chisel and 2-pound hammer, or—best of all—a power-driven impact chisel.)

For many years I have encountered a widespread impression that wood should be avoided for use in bathrooms because it reacts badly to humidity and water and quickly warps and rots. Many wooden-walled nineteenth-century bathrooms still in good condition confirm the opposite.* Many, of course, are also in sad state, but a close look at these usually shows that it is the finish rather than the wood itself that has deteriorated and one need feel no hesitation in using wood for some or all the bathroom walls.

Left unfinished, wood will develop a patina of toothpaste, soap splatters, and discolored areas caused by cycles of wetting and drying. (Exotic types of woods such as lignum vitae that contain large amounts of oil are exceptions.) Ordinary maintenance requires a finish over the wood that will not permit staining material to penetrate. The simplest and cheapest finish is two or more coats of polyurethane. I have used various brands of polyurethane and found them all alike though prices ranged between from $4 to $12 a gallon. I have for many years bought only the cheapest and found results equal to the use of more expensive brands. One gallon covers 350 square feet on the first coat and 600 square feet on additional coats. More than three coats is counterproductive. One can expect a polyurethane finish in the bathroom to last six years or longer before recoating is desirable.

Applying polyurethane directly to a planed board will often result in blotched areas around knots and

*Indeed, if you go to England, you will find toilets whose bowls and tanks are framed in wood, in beautiful condition, and doubtless date back to the reign of Queen Victoria.

other imperfections due to nicks, gouges, and furry spots on the surface that the planer has not removed. To produce a fine finish, one that will truly prevent absorption of staining material and shed water, each board will have to be sanded at least eight times, beginning with 80 grit paper on a belt sander and increasingly fine paper on successive passes, completing the process with 400 grit paper on an orbital sander. One may, of course, stop sanding at any intermediate point, but the best finish requires going the entire route.

After the sanding process is completed, the wood is almost dense enough along its surface to resist water penetration even without polyurethane. Three coats of polyurethane provides an optimum finish. (I built a bathroom with solid mahogany ceiling and walls treated in the manner described and it is still in excellent condition nineteen years later.)

A good practice is to seal the bottom end of each board with resin and hardener epoxy (A and B) to prevent absorption into the end grain of the wood, its most vulnerable area.

A neat installation is achieved around the tub through the use of tub mold, a chrome strip factory-contoured to fit the shape of the tub. A thin metal extension is provided for nailing to cats installed in the walls just above the top of the tub. After cats are installed, a heavy bead of silicone caulking is laid between the tub top and cats and mold nailed over it. The bottom edge of the mold fits against the tub and the caulking behind it prevents water from being sloshed through to the framework. The mold eliminates an unsightly seam of grout or caulking and one sees only a thin strip of chrome that wipes clean easily.

The ends of wood paneling butt the top edge of the mold and are subjected to a good deal of water. Each of these ends should receive two coats of A and B epoxy.

To prevent water from passing through joints between boards, paneling should be tongue-and-groove if installed vertically. Installed horizontally, board may be ship-lapped. A good practice is to coat joints heavily with polyurethane just prior to installation. All nailheads should be countersunk and holes filled with color-matched stick putty to avoid nail bleeding.

At 17 cents per board foot, wood treated as

described makes an excellent and durable wall. (Maple is a particularly good hardwood to use and will withstand heavy wear and tear if finished properly.)

Installing Ceramic Tile on Bathroom Walls

If not already installed, cats should be nailed between studs just above the top of the tub to provide nailing surfaces for the lower ends of the sheetrock and tub mold. Walls should also be framed for such recessed fixtures as soap dishes,* toilet-paper holder, medicine chest, and all other items to be contained within the walls. Rough openings vary but all manufacturers provide the necessary dimensions.

If a wall-hung basin is projected, a 1-×-12 cleat is installed in the bay behind it flush with the studs. The lower edge of the cleat is 26 inches above the finished floor height. The cleat provides a surface to attach a hanger bar on which the basin is mounted.

I nail aluminum edging in corners between the tub and ceiling to prevent water from reaching the framework. (Edging is the same as that used for the roof.) Although tile is waterproof, grout used to fill joints is not. Corner joints are particularly susceptible to the development of cracks and the use of edging is a good, cheap precaution.

I install water-resistant sheetrock (usually colored green) over the walls as previously described for ordinary sheetrock. I lay a heavy bead of silicone caulking along the joint between the top of the tub and cats and nail tub mold over it.

I pop level chalk lines on the walls ³/₁₆ inch below the finished floor height and temporarily nail scrap strips of wood along the lines. The strips provide a level reference for the lowest course of tile and also prevent them from slipping down when first installed. (Once mastic has dried, it maintains tiles without support.) The thickness of ordinary mosaic floor tile is ³/₁₆ inch and by placing the wall tiles below, allowance is made for both to be flush after installation of the floor tile.

*Put them out of the way of falling water if shower-takers who don't like soggy soap will be the primary users of the bathroom.

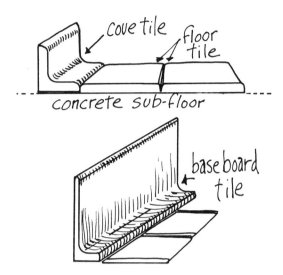

The bottom course of tile may be either L-shaped baseboard tile or cove.

Baseboard tile is manufactured in the same color as wall tile but contrasting colors are also frequently used. The tile has a built-in cove (curved surface) to make cleaning easier.

Cove tile is also manufactured in many colors and types. Special pieces are provided for exterior and interior corners. Because of their small size, cove pieces are more difficult to align but make a smoother and less obvious joint.

Mastic is manufactured as water-resistant and waterproof. Water-resistant types should be avoided since their resistance to water is nonexistent, and they dissolve with ordinary use. Mastic sells for about $5 per gallon. Waterproof mastic performs well and costs about $12 per gallon. (Two gallons of mastic will be needed.)

Mastic is applied to the wall with notched trowels or notched spreaders. (Either type is usually supplied free with the purchase of mastic.) Gasoline or turpentine is a good solvent, but its use should be limited to cleaning and not to thinning mastic. Mastic containers should be kept covered when not in use to avoid inhaling fumes and to prevent evaporation of the highly volatile and inflammable solvent. Mastic that gets on tile surfaces should be wiped clean within fifteen minutes or so with a rag wetted in gasoline. If allowed to dry, mastic is hard to remove.

Once applied to the wall, mastic dries fairly quickly; the amount spread at any one time should not exceed the amount of tile one can lay within fifteen or twenty minutes. If at any time work has to be suspended, all unused mastic should be removed. Mastic that has been allowed to dry on the wall will not permit flat placement of tiles and its removal is a laborious and needless chore.

I use a notched trowel (it deposits a uniform thickness) to spread mastic along the area to be covered by baseboard tiles. I start in a corner with a corner baseboard tile that is shaped in a right angle and has a surface on each intersecting wall.

Wall tiles are manufactured with slight pips on all sides that extend a bit less than $1/16$ inch. As tiles are butted to each other, a gap is automatically created and will later be filled with grout. Baseboard tiles do not have pips and I use book matches as spacers. I lay each baseboard tile against the mastic and butt its bottom against the level cleat.

I install baseboard tiles in the same manner until I am less than the width of a tile from the second corner. I install the second corner tile.

I measure the gap between the installed baseboard and corner tile and mark another baseboard tile $1/8$ inch narrower (to allow for grout joints).

I use the pictured tile cutter to cut along the desired line. This tool is essentially a glass cutter mounted on an arm that slides along a rigid bar. Tile cutters retail under $12 and pay for themselves in labor saved even if used for only one bathroom.

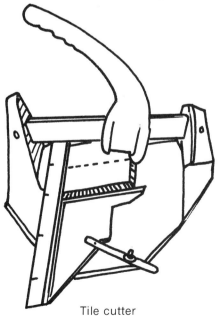

Tile cutter

To cut tile, the following sequence is recommended:

1. Place a pencil mark on the edge of the tile at the desired cut. The mark needn't be continued across the tile.

2. Lift the handle and slide it back completely.

3. Place the tile on the rubber pad and align the pencil mark at the V on the ruled scale. (If more than one tile of the same dimension is to be cut, loosen the wing nut, slide the fence, and butt it to the tile; retighten the wing nut; and place all successive tiles against the fence.)

4. Pull up the handle and lay the cutting wheel on the mark. Hold the tile stationary with the left hand.

5. Press down with enough force to create a scratching sound and push the handle forward across the face of the tile. The surface should be scored by a faint line. If no scratching sound is heard, the line isn't being scored and increased pressure should be applied. If increased pressure doesn't result in the scratching sound, the cutting wheel is dull and should be replaced. (A single screw holds it.)

6. Lower the handle, slide it back until the butterfly-shaped piece behind the wheel is centered over the scored line, raise the handle, and swing it down. As the butterfly strikes the tile, a raised metal bar directly under the scored line assists the action and the tile breaks along the scored line. The force used to strike the tile is equivalent to a moderate tap.

Occasionally the tile doesn't break. Examine the scored line. Only a surface scratch is required, but if the scratch is intermittent, it should be rescored. If the tile still doesn't break after rescoring, place it face down in the left hand and tap its back along the line with increasing force until it does. From time to time the tile breaks along an undesired line; such losses are to be expected about 1 percent of the time. Whenever possible, I recut pieces for use elsewhere.

I install the cut baseboard tile in the gap near the second corner and complete the baseboard course along the remaining walls in the same manner.

I pop a plumb vertical chalk line 4 $5/16$ inches out from the first corner and install tiles at the line to ensure verticality. I maintain one side of the tile at the chalk line and trim the side in the corner if necessary. (The corner itself may not be plumb.) The trimmed edge in the corner will be hidden by tiles on the intersecting wall.

I spread mastic in a 2-foot-square area near the corner, butting tiles to the baseboard and to each other. Baseboard tiles are ordinarily wider than wall tiles and joints cannot be aligned.

I am installing partial courses in the 2-foot square and *do not* extend any tile farther toward the opposite wall than the tile below it. Each tile is installed by laying it into the mastic and positioning it against adjacent tiles. Pips provide uniform gaps.

I nail a 1-inch-wide batten butted to the ceiling. Its thickness is the same as the tile and will serve as a nailing surface for molding to cover the joint between the top course and ceiling. (Molding is optional; tiles can be continued to the ceiling and the joint filled with grout.)

I continue to lay tiles until I reach the bottom of the batten. I intend the molding to be 1 3/8 inches wide, and the fit between its lower side and the tile needn't be tight since the joint will be hidden.

I select a straight 1 × 3, mark the joints between tiles in it, and then transfer the marks to the opposite corner. The new marks are used as references to align each course horizontally and maintain them in a level plane across the wall. The marks also ensure that all courses of tile will meet in corners at the same height. (If necessary, slightly larger gaps are used to bring a course back to a level plane.)

Pipes emerge from the wall at each fixture and tile must be cut around them. The fit needn't be tight since an escutcheon plate around the pipe is at least 1 inch larger than the diameter of the pipe and will hide irregularities and gaps. (If the gap is very large, larger escutcheons are easily obtainable at any plumbing supply house.)

The drawing shows a masonry-cutting blade and Skil saw positioned for use in cutting tile. The guard of the saw is held back by wedging a piece of wood between it and the housing. The saw is then turned upside down and the left hand used to depress the trigger. The right hand slides the tile along the table and gently into the turning blade. It is important to feed the tile slowly since excessive forward pressure often causes the tile to break along undesired lines. Cutting tile with a tile cutter is appropriate only when the desired cut is a single

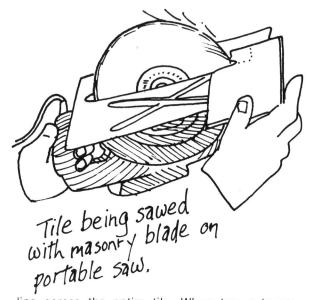

Tile being sawed with masonry blade on portable saw.

line across the entire tile. When two cuts are needed, as in notching around pipes, a composition blade and Skil saw are optimum.

When cutting a notch in tile, the piece being removed sometimes breaks before cuts are completed and leaves a ragged edge. If the excess material is relatively large, it is removed with an additional cut. If the excess material is merely ragged, it is smoothed to a straight line by *very gently* laying the ragged edge against the side of the turning blade. A composition blade has little lateral strength and, if tile is pressed too strongly against it, may shatter. (I have trimmed many tile edges in this manner and have never had a blade shatter.)

When a pipe falls entirely within a single tile, several methods of cutting the required hole are possible; none is particularly satisfactory and the tile is best installed in two pieces with a visible crack.

At each end of the tub, its top and side form a curve and the mold follows the contour. Tiles along the curves must also be cut to the same shape. To do this, I mark the curve on the back of the tile (cutting from the front chips the glaze), then saw a series of straight parallel lines with the composition blade so that each cut ends at a point along the arc. I remove ragged edges by passing them laterally and *gently* across the cutting edge of the blade. It is *essential that only a slight bit of material is removed with each pass* so that the danger of the blade catching the tile and flinging it away is avoided.

After all the tile has been installed, the mastic should be allowed to dry overnight before further work is done.

The gaps between tiles are to be filled with a finely ground cement called grout. Grout used by itself often develops cracks; a good practice is to add a handful of very fine sand to five pounds of grout. The practice reduces cracking but does not eliminate it. (Vinyl grout is superior to ordinary grout and a good deal more expensive. It doesn't eliminate cracking but reduces the incidence to a tolerable level.)

I mix five pounds of vinyl grout and water in a clean plastic bucket to a consistency of toothpaste. I spread the grout over the tile with a rubber-faced trowel and force it into all joints with moderate pressure. I allow the grout to set for half an hour, then run a wet sponge *lightly* across the surface of the tile to remove excess grout. (It is important to keep the pressure light and avoid forcing water into the joints since this will weaken the bonds between particles of grout.) I rinse the sponge often. I wait another half hour and repeat. Toward the end of the day, I run a damp rag over the tile. The following morning a white film will have formed and can be removed with a dry rag.

Excess grout is removed before it has had time to dry. Grout that has been permitted to dry is laborious and time-consuming to remove.

Ceramic soap dishes, toilet paper holders, and the like are installed with the same mastic used for tiles. It works well except for the soap dish of the tub that has a grab bar and is subjected to greater stress. If the dish comes loose, it can be reinstalled more securely in the following manner:

I cram newspaper into the hollow behind the r.o. until solid and a gap of a couple of inches remains between the sheetrock and paper. I mix two fistfuls of plaster of Paris with water to the consistency of butter at room temperature and heap it on the back of the dish. I immediately insert the dish into the opening and press it forward to the wall. The plaster on the back is spread beyond the r.o. and forms a large and powerful key. I maintain the pressure and *do not shift the dish for at least a minute.* Plaster of Paris hardens within a few minutes and if shifted during its setting time loses its strength. In ten minutes or so, I scrape off the excess plaster and smooth the joints with a spackling knife.

FLOORS

6

Until recently, wood was the most widely used flooring material in dwellings, bathrooms and kitchens excepted. Yellow pine, fir, maple, walnut, and other hardwoods, formerly a significant source, have gradually given way to the nearly exclusive use of either red or white oak. Oak is resilient, durable, hard enough to resist marring, easily installed, and lends itself to mass construction because of widespread availability. It is a poor conductor of heat with good insulating characteristics and (most important) provides a warm and comfortable surface to walk on. Oak has the disadvantage of requiring periodic refinishing, but this aspect did not overly concern builders and until the late 1960s was used in even low-priced homes.

Standard oak flooring is sold in random lengths (rarely longer than 4 feet or shorter than 1 foot). Sides are tongue-and-grooved and ends matched; also tongue-and-grooved and cut squarely to provide a tight joint. Standard thickness is $^{25}/_{32}$ inch. Standard width is 1 × 3 for selling purposes but only 2 $^{1}/_{4}$ inches remain exposed. In the late sixties, oak flooring sold for $210 per thousand; the cost is now $800. Since a thousand board feet covers only 700 square feet of floor, the effective cost of oak is more than $1 per square foot of floor area to be covered, and far too expensive for the addition.

Planed 1-×-3 oak can be purchased at a sawmill for an effective cost of 25 cents per square foot of floor area to be covered and is a viable material for the addition. However, the sides and ends will have to be milled, a technique that has already been described. (Four carbide-tipped bits will be needed since the end joints are different from the side joints.)

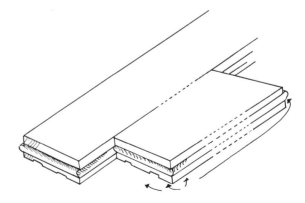

Tongue-and-groove sides and ends of flooring

Oak is a harder wood to mill than softwoods; to obtain the pictured joints a 1 1/2-horsepower router is minimal and a more powerful one preferable. For approximately 6 cents a lineal foot, joints can be milled commercially. Even with this additional cost, oak is still viable for the addition.

After milling, oak should be stacked inside the addition and allowed to dry for several months. Drying time is reduced to six weeks or so if the addition is heated. An alternative is to have the oak dried in a commercial kiln at about 2 cents per foot. (Kilns are normally located within a short distance of sawmills.)

A superior alternative is to construct a small solar kiln that receives all its energy from the sun. Kilns of this type can by constructed in less than a day and the Department of the Interior supplies plans for them free of charge. (I've examined wood dried in a homemade kiln and found it as good as wood dried commercially.)

The standard method of installing oak flooring is to lay pieces end to end in a straight line from wall to wall. It is certainly the quickest way, but I find the installation hopelessly bland. It is a method that best suits commercial use, but when I make a considerable effort to obtain and prepare oak I want better than standard as a result.

Shown are four common ways to lay flooring other than in straight lines. Many other ways can be seen in books devoted to architectural history and design and newer variations in brochures prepared by the Hardwood Institute, flooring companies, interior design magazines, and quite often in better lumber yards.

A combination of oak and darker hardwoods such as walnut is used for greater enhancement and definition of each. In some installations, 1-by-3-inch (or narrower) strips of darkwood are laid singly or in a wide band around the perimeter of the room. Some floors employ alternate squares of light and dark hardwood laid parallel or diagonally; others divide the floor into large squares with walnut strips and fill their interiors with oak. Still others employ a Greek-key design in mahogany around the perimeter. In some installations the oak flooring is continued up the walls for several inches to form a baseboard. A great many other designs exist or can be created for a unique and personal floor.

Herringbone

Parquet

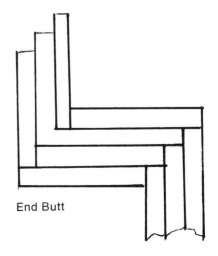

End Butt

Maple is another excellent material for flooring and can be purchased at a sawmill for the same price as oak and used in all the previously described ways. It may also be milled into 1 × 2s (bowling-alley floors) or wide planks for a completely different appearance; 1 × 2s are easiest to lay but many more pieces are involved and erase the advantage. It is also about 15 percent more expensive than a standard installation since surface exposure is further reduced by the greater number of joints.

All wide boards are relatively difficult to align and maple is no exception. Practice shows that if 1 × 3s are used and a gap exists between pieces, it will not be too difficult to close. If 1 × 4s are being used, closing gaps will be a good deal harder; if boards are wider, a standard installation isn't practical and the boards will have to be installed in another manner by the technique called pegging, detailed later in the chapter. No skill or expensive tools are required, and laying a maple (or other wood) plank floor is actually less costly and involves no more work than a standard 1-×-3 installation.

If hardwood isn't available at a viable cost, white pine or fir are adequate though not such good substitutes. (They are softer and scar more easily.)

With the steep rise in cost of wood flooring, vinyl, rubber, vinyl asbestos, and other composition materials have come into widespread use and are available in tile or sheet form. The cheapest of these products, and also the most durable, is vinyl asbestos that sells for about 25 cents per square foot. It can be laid directly on the slab. (If vinyl asbestos is projected, the surface of the slab is smoothed with a steel trowel.) When economy is the sole objective, vinyl asbestos tile is the optimum choice. One can expect the tile to last upward of ten years, but maintenance is laborious and ongoing. Colors and designs are extremely limited and among the ugliest of flooring products.

Other types of composition tile or linoleum require either burdensome maintenance or costs begin at about $1 per square foot and are too expensive to consider. (Cushioned vinyl sheets are particularly bad since they leave indentations from chairs, heels, and so on that supposedly disappear but often do not.) The practice of using particle board and carpet is also to be avoided since the installation is relatively expensive, has a short life, and vacuuming is an ongoing chore.

The addition floor is presently concrete and provides an excellent base for many suitable masonry products. Commercially obtained masonry products are too expensive to consider, but many of the same products are available elsewhere at a fraction of the cost or at no cost at all.

Slate is one of these products. Unlike its use on edge for walls, where backing is required, slate on a floor is laid in a bed of mortar directly on the concrete and joints filled with natural or colored mortar. An inexperienced person should expect to spend a week or so to lay the floor, compared to a day if wood is used. The additional labor will result in a permanent floor that is easily maintained and has a highly attractive appearance. The only cost involved is about $15 for cement, cream, and sand.

Slate, like all masonry materials, has no resilience and is a ''hard'' floor to walk on. Unless the addition is in a warm climate, the floor is cold and uncomfortable in socks or bare feet during winter. Its irregular surface causes furniture to rock, and additional work to level particular areas should be expected. These inconveniences are often eliminated by the use of rugs to cover parts of the floor. All in all, the advantages of a slate floor far outweigh minor inconveniences and slate is thus an excellent choice.

Split stone, like slate, is also free and a prime flooring material. Unlike slate, it is rarely used, and my own experience is limited to a decorative wall patch and a floor I laid many years ago. (I renovated a monastery in Corsica that had a fabulous-looking split-stone floor that inspired me.) Vertical distances should be held to a maximum of 6 inches in order to keep the finished height of the floor from being raised excessively. Faces should be held within 2 feet to keep from using stone too heavy to manipulate. Installation time can be expected to be about a week.

Joints between split-stone pieces tend to become wide, since perimeters are curved rather than linear. Excessively wide joints are reduced by laying smaller stones in them.

There is no way of knowing what the interior color or texture of the stone will be before it is split, and one has to be prepared to discard pieces that do not fit into the projected design. A good practice is to assemble all the pieces on the floor in their intended arrangement before installation is begun.

If the goal is an economical, unusual, and highly personal floor that is both permanent and easily maintained, split stone is a superior material to use.

Used brick is another masonry product that makes a fine floor. (New brick at 16 cents each is prohibitively expensive.) On many occasions I have bought used brick at a demolition site for 2 cents each and in several instances had them given to me at no cost. I had to transport the bricks and remove old mortar at my own expense. Though totally different in appearance from stone, brick has all the same practical advantages and a very considerable disadvantage of being much more difficult to lay. Before a decision to use brick is made, one should understand that laying a tolerably flat floor and aligning bricks is time-consuming, though not beyond the capacity of an inexperienced person. (There is a house on the road between Grass Valley and Auburn in California with bricks laid in the shape of an S on its side. This kind of installation is simpler than aligning bricks lineally.) The most important factor in making a choice is the final appearance, so if brick is most pleasing, no hesitation need be felt about using it. During laying, a string is simply stretched between level bricks at opposite ends of the room and each successive brick laid to the string. Joints are later filled with mortar. Skill will only make the installation time shorter and inexperience longer.

Tile is another masonry product that provides an excellent floor and fulfills the requirements of permanence and ease of maintenance. Quarry tile is standard (the tiles aren't quarried; the word refers to the thickness of the tile, $3/8$ to $3/4$ inch). Since the floor is concrete and the tile will be embedded in masonry rather than glued with mastic, any thickness is suitable. Tiles with a smooth, glazed finish should be avoided to eliminate the hazard of slipping.

Unless one is prepared to spend 70 cents per square foot and upward to $5 or more, the usual route of obtaining tile at a store or lumber or masonry yard should be abandoned. Reasonably priced alternate sources are wrecking yards, flea markets, and occasionally retailers or wholesalers

with small amounts of new tile remaining from discontinued types. I have bought tile at all four places at prices under 40 cents per square foot, a viable cost for the addition.

Quarry tile is ordinarily manufactured without a glaze and presents a maintenance problem since it absorbs spills and stains. Liquid sealers that coat the surface and supposedly make them impervious are readily available but *do not* perform as advertised. Within a few weeks or months of normal use, the sealer is worn away—leaving a whitish discoloration—and a new coat is required. The use of wax and other coatings only exacerbates the problem and turns maintenance into a continuous and onerous chore. Glazed quarry tiles (small amounts are manufactured) with an uneven rather than flat surface is the type that best fulfills the requirements of a good floor.

Porcelain tile is vitreous, which means that its greater density allows very little absorption and resists staining adequately without the use of a glaze. Its colors are a result of stains and oxides baked with the tile and are permanent. It is usually manufactured in small sizes and referred to as mosaic tile for that reason. To ease installation, backing is placed on the face or back of tiles to join them into a single sheet (usually 1 foot square). Face-backing consists of paper and a water-soluble glue that is removed by wetting. Backing on the back is usually a plastic mesh with more than enough surface for the tiles to adhere and doesn't require removal.

A familiar variety of porcelain tile is white and hexagonal, a favorite material for bathroom floors in older apartment buildings. (Many porcelain-tile floors, seventy years old and older, are still in excellent condition.) Other varieties of mosaic tile are variously colored 1-inch squares, also long-lasting and easily maintained. Since both types are cheapest, it is unrealistic to expect to find them in used condition at a reduced price and I would limit their use to the bathroom floor, where the area to be covered is only 30 square feet or so.

Mosaic tile may be installed with floor-tile adhesive over an underlayment of particle board, plywood, or Masonite. None of these is recommended since water passes through the grouted joints and causes the underlayment to warp and rot. It is also relatively expensive, and if marine plywood (a type that is truly waterproof) is used costs go up even further. The best installation (and incidentally the cheapest) is to lay the tile in a masonry bed for a permanent and trouble-free floor.

Installing 1-×-3 Oak Flooring, End to End

I spread plastic roof cement over the slab with a notched trowel in a 3-foot swath from wall to opposite wall and lay 15-pound felt (tar paper) over it. I cover the entire slab with felt. The felt is a vapor barrier that blocks moisture from the slab. (If flooring is laid directly on the slab or felt, even the small amount of humidity that passes through causes the oak to expand and the floor to buckle.)

I now need to build a wooden framework on the slab that will bring the finished floor height of the addition flush with the existing floor in the house. I measure the distance between the felt and finished floor, subtract 3/4 inch to allow for the thickness of the oak (actually 25/32 inch), and obtain the required height.

Several arrangements are possible to achieve the desired height. For example, let us say that after allowing for the thickness of the oak, the assembly needs to lie 5 3/4 inches above the slab.

A standard arrangement is illustrated. If necessary, I can provide additional height by laying the lowest 2 × 4s on edge rather than flat or use 2 × 6s, 2 × 8s, and so on if even more height is required. (If 2 × 6s are used, they are spaced 6 feet apart; 2 × 8s are put 8 feet apart.) If necessary I can lower the height by using 1 × 3s on the flat rather than 2 × 4s and for smaller amounts 1/2 inch or 5/8-inch subfloor material.

Members that lie on the felt are coated with tar for adhesion and needn't be nailed to the slab.

A decision needs to be made about insulating the floor before the subfloor is nailed. In this situation, the use of fiberglass or any other type of insulation is counterproductive. The amount of heat loss through the floor is negligible, and not only is insulation a needless expense but also a liability because it provides surfaces for condensation to accumulate and causes a humid condition under the floor. The dead-air spaces already present are excellent insulators and permit condensation to be reabsorbed by the slab and dissipated.

The use of thin plastic sheets under the subfloor as a vapor barrier causes relatively large amounts of condensation and should not be used. (On the insistence of a "heating expert," I once installed 3-mil plastic sheets over studs before paneling the walls. Several days later water was seeping from the walls and I was obliged to remove the paneling and rip out the plastic sheets.)

To reduce humidity even further and eliminate squeaks caused by the oak rubbing against the subfloor, I install an additional layer of felt over the subfloor.

I pop a chalk line 3 inches from either wall that lies at a right angle to the joists. By following the line during the first course rather than butting pieces against the wall, I ensure a straight line. I pop chalk lines on the tar paper that correspond to the centers of joists. I lay oak pieces end to end from wall to opposite wall and mark the positions of joists on the oak. I clip the head off a # 6 finishing nail and use it as a bit to bore holes in the oak at joist locations. Each hole is positioned 1/2 inch from the grooved side. I nail oak pieces along the chalk

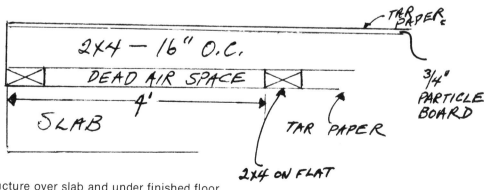

Substructure over slab and under finished floor

line with #8 finishing nails driven through the predrilled holes into joists.

After sawing the last piece for the first course, I use the remainder to start the second course. (If the remainder is less than 4 inches, it should be discarded.)

I place all pieces of the second course end to end and drill holes at a toenail angle through the joint directly at the top of the tongue. I use a rubber mallet to position pieces of the second course against the first and nail with finishing nails through the predrilled holes.

A helper lays out successive courses behind me. The helper should try to minimize waste and stagger joints between pieces so that they do not accumulate in the same area.

I rent a manually operated flooring machine that is available for a modest cost at most lumber yards or tool-rental establishments. The machine uses special nails joined in clips. (One box provides enough nails for 1000 square feet of flooring.) Clips are loaded into a slot at the side of the machine. The machine is positioned on the oak along the tongue and its rocker arm struck forcibly with a leather mallet (provided with machine). The nail is automatically located above the tongue and driven flush with the wood. (There is not enough room to use the machine for the first two courses.)

I continue to lay each course with the machine until I am within two or possibly three courses from the opposite wall, where the distance is too narrow to continue using it. I nail the remaining courses in the same manner as the first two courses to complete the installation.

Oak flooring is generally straight because of its short lengths and pieces come together nicely during nailing. Occasionally one encounters a curved piece. If the gap is less than 1/4 inch, it can usually be eliminated by additional nailing. If this isn't successful, the gap is removed by nailing half of a diagonal piece of flooring beside it and driving the other half as a wedge. If the gap is larger than 1/4 inch, the piece should be cut at the curve and installed as two pieces.

Finishing an oak floor is a process that begins with sanding to remove variations in height, scratches, nicks and to transform a relatively rough and porous surface into a smooth, densely packed one. A drum sander and edger are two machines needed; both are available for rental at hardware stores and lumber yards. A hook scraper is also needed and sells for less than $2.

The drum sander has a rubber-sheathed revolving drum over which the sandpaper is attached. The machine cannot sand adjacent to walls or in corners because of its housing. The better drum sanders use 240 volts rather than 120 and should be sought out because of their superior performance.

The edger is a smaller machine that reaches all areas the drum sander cannot, except for a small patch in each corner. The edger uses circular sandpaper discs and rotates at high speed. The hook scraper is used in those areas that are inaccessible to the edger.

Sandpaper for use with the machines is either open or closed-coat. Open-coat papers are used to remove old varnish, paint, or large variations in height. (Abrasive particles are impregnated intermittently; a 20 grit open-coat paper, for example, has 20 abrasive particles per square inch.) Particles are contiguous in closed-coat paper. Since we are dealing here with new wood and slight variations in height, only closed-coat paper is used.

Sandpaper is a great deal less expensive if purchased by the roll. A roll will sand 7000 square feet of flooring. The quality of this sandpaper is also far better than ordinarily encountered.

If a roll isn't purchased, eight precut sheets of closed-coat paper should be obtained for the drum sander: three medium coarse, two medium fine, and three fine. Six discs will be needed for the edger; three each of medium fine and fine. This is enough sandpaper for a good finish but if a superior one is desired, four additional sheets of very fine paper and two very fine discs will be needed.

Just below the right side of the wooden handle of the drum sander is a forked metal handle that controls the position of the drum. To raise the drum off the floor, the fork is squeezed together, pulled back and up, and released. To lower the drum, the fork is squeezed together, pushed forward and down, and released.

To attach a sheet of sandpaper, I raise the drum off the floor. On each side are two square nutlike projections that control two metal bars in the interior. The drum has a slot across its width through which the bars can be seen. When viewed from an end, the bars are seen to be shaped like a marble cut in half. I rotate the bars by turning the square nuts with the supplied wrenches so that the flat sides face one another. I insert one end of the sheet into the drum slot with its abrasive side facing out and push it between the bars as far as it will go. I rotate the drum till the slot reappears and pull the paper tightly to the drum. I fold the remaining end (without creasing it), insert it into the slot, and push it forward until all slack is removed. I cut a strip of cardboard 1 inch wide and slightly shorter than the length of the slot. The thickness of the cardboard should be roughly the same as the sandpaper. I insert the cardboard between the sandpaper in the slot and press it forward until it lies flush. (The purpose of the cardboard is to force the sandpaper tightly against the drum *before* the bars are adjusted.) I place one wrench on the square nut at my right and another on the left, pull up on the right wrench, and simultaneously push down on the left. This turns the rounded portion of the bars to an inward position, secures the paper, and tightens it a bit more against the drum.

Many sheets are often torn in the first few seconds of use because the sandpaper has not been sufficiently tightened against the drum. The action of the bars tightens the sheet to only a small degree, and unless the paper is snug before they are rotated all slack will not be removed.

Exposed nails are countersunk and debris removed from the room before sanding.

I begin with a medium coarse sheet. Before starting the machine, I drape its cable over my shoulders and around the back of my neck and *raise the drum off the floor.* The single most common cause of a poor finishing job is permitting the drum to rotate on the floor while the sander is in a stationary position. *The machine must be kept in constant motion while sanding is being done or a gouge will be made.*

I position the machine so that I can comfortably guide it toward the diagonally opposite corner. (Contrary to popular belief that one always sands with the grain, diagonal sanding is more effective in achieving a flat surface.) I switch on the machine and begin to push it forward. *While the sander is moving, I lower the drum gently onto the floor and continue moving ahead.* The powerful drum requires no forward pressure and I only guide it. If the machine self-propels itself too quickly, I use a bit of

back pressure to slow it. The pace should not be faster than a stroll. As the front of the machine approaches within 2 feet of the corner, I seize the forked handle and raise the drum from the floor while the machine is still moving. I turn the machine around and make a parallel pass adjacent to the first in the same manner. I continue making passes on one side of the diagonal until the length of a pass is too short to be effective. I repeat the process on the opposite side of the diagonal.

I now run the drum sander around the perimeter of the room and keep the machine close to the walls. When sanding with the grain, wood is removed more slowly and I hold back lightly. When sanding against the grain, I use no back pressure to avoid excessive removal of wood.

A ribbon several inches wide around the perimeter of the room remains to be sanded. (There are also patches in corners.) The edger used to sand the ribbon turns at a much higher speed than the drum and revolves on a vertical rather than horizontal axis. This causes the edger to produce a different surface than that left by the drum, even if the sandpaper is identical. The difference becomes less noticeable as finer paper is used and very fine papers remove it entirely. For this reason, and because the amount of material to be removed is relatively small, I use closed-coat, medium fine sandpaper on the edger during the first pass.

The edger is switched on with its rear tilted back slightly and the disc up from the floor. (Part of the front housing is cut away and the disc is visible.)

The edger has casters. I slide it against the wall, then back and forth over the floor while still in contact with the wall. If it is necessary to return to a particular spot for resanding after the initial pass, I slide the edger back and forth several feet beyond the spot. Wide passes are needed to prevent oversanding. This technique is called feathering and applies to the drum sander as well.

The edger must be kept flat on its casters. A tilt will cause the disc to cut into the flooring and a deep gouge can occur in a fraction of a second. The edger should not be kept stationary at any time and sweeps are wide lateral strokes performed on the quicker side, even if this requires several additional passes over the same area.

To use the hook scraper, my left hand lies slightly behind the cutting blade and supplies moderate downward pressure. My right hand grips the handle and pulls the blade toward me. Scraping is done on the pulling stroke. The scraper is then lifted and reset. When scrapers are slid forward on the floor, their cutting edges dull rapidly. Even with proper use, the edge becomes dull after ten minutes or so of use. The cutting edge is resharpened by running a mill bastard file on its bevel two or three times.

I make a minimum of eight complete passes over the entire floor in the manner described and use increasingly fine paper.

I have a number of cosmetic options at this point. If a darker floor is desired, I apply an oil stain of appropriate color by brushing and wiping with a rag. The longer the stain is allowed to remain on the oak, the darker the appearance. I allow the stain to dry overnight. If a lighter floor is desired, I use a half-and-half mixture of white, oil-based paint and turpentine that produces a whitish translucent film and sharp definition of the grain. Again, the longer the mixture is allowed to remain on the oak before wiping it off with a rag, the whiter the result.

If a stain is to be applied, I prepare a paste of stain, fine sawdust, and epoxy glue and fill nicks, gaps, and nailholes. After allowing several hours for drying, I vacuum the room and wipe the entire surface with a rag that has been dampened in denatured alcohol to remove finer particles of sawdust left after vacuuming. I shut the windows to keep foreign material from blowing onto the floor, remove my shoes to avoid leaving marks, and am ready to apply the final finish.

Polyurethane is by far the optimum material to coat the surface. It is available in a satin or high-gloss finish. Prices vary from $4 to $14 per gallon. I always obtain the cheapest since I have found that the results are as good as with the highest-priced brands. Two gallons will be needed.

Polyurethane is applied with either a 4-inch varnish brush or a short-haired roller. The brush gives better results but the roller is much quicker. I use both, the roller attached to an extension pole for the main spreading and the brush for removing spatters, runs, drips, and for reaching areas inaccessible to the roller.

To increase penetration into the oak, on the first coat only I thin a gallon of polyurethane with a pint of turpentine. I pour part of the mixture into a paint pan to a level just below the metal arm at the side of the roller so that the liquid will not get on the arm and drip on the floor as I shift the roller from the pan to the work area. After dipping the roller, I remove excess polyurethane by rolling it lightly over the ridges at the back of the pan.

I begin at the corner farthest from the exit, swing the roller gently from the pan to the floor, and begin a stroke about 3 feet from where I intend the swath to end. I push the roller forward, pull it back 6 feet or so, then return over the swath to the starting point. I stroke with the grain throughout.

I pass the roller over the floor, using a trifle more pressure than that created by the weight of the roller. Heavier pressure is a frequent cause of a bad job since the liquid is squeezed out the sides of the roller and accumulates in a heavy streak. When heavy pressure and excessive speed are used, bubbles become trapped in the liquid. Dry bubbles are punctured after being walked on and leave a whitish ring around their edges. A slow, deliberate, light stroke is essential.

If spatters occur and drops are allowed to dry, the exposed surface of the drop forms a crust while the liquid within it remains wet. When the drop is walked on and the crust broken, the semi-liquid polyurethane inside leaves a smear. After I complete each patch, I check the surface for bubbles and drops and remove them with the brush before continuing.

Throughout the application, I use floorboards as a reference and overlap passes for an inch or so along the sides and several inches along the ends since less urethane is deposited in these areas than elsewhere.

It is both unnecessary and undesirable to run the roller over a swath more than one time. One pass done with light pressure is sufficient to deposit an adequate thickness of film.

After fifteen minutes or so, drying polyurethane develops spots without a sheen; these appear to have no liquid over them when in fact they do. The lack of sheen is due to the greater porosity in that particular spot. (If doubt exists, touch the spot.) There is no need to go over these areas and one should expect to see them, particularly on the first coat.

If the application is done in cold and wet weather, a minimum of twenty-four hours should be allowed between coats. If the weather is hot and dry, drying time should be overnight. To determine the state of the polyurethane, pierce the dry-to-the-touch coat with an awl and note if the tip is sticky.

When the first coat has dried, it has a slight roughness due to dust and the nap of the wood (small wood fibers that have been drawn erect on the surface). Ordinary use wears away a good deal of the roughness but may also permit entry of liquids and premature deterioration. A single coat will last only a couple of years before evidencing significant signs of wear.

When more than one coat is to be applied, manufacturers recommend fine sanding between coats to ensure a bond and to remove foreign materials lodged in the first coat. When I first began using polyurethane, I fine-sanded between coats but found that I obtained equally satisfactory results without sanding. By cleaning the floor meticulously before the first coat and by keeping it clean throughout the application, nap and foreign particles became a negligible factor.

However, when sanding between coats is omitted, *it is essential that the polyurethane not be allowed to dry for more than twenty-four hours before the next coat is applied.* Because twenty-four hours is too great a variable depending on temperature, humidity, air circulation and the like, I have adopted the procedure of applying the second coat twelve hours or so after the first. It has worked in a variety of climatic situations and with a great many applications.

After twelve hours of drying, the floor is not ready for heavy use but can be walked on. It is also wet enough to bond to the second coat.

If more than twenty-four hours has elapsed, I use a steel-wool pad on a rotary buffer to remove the nap and dust and faintly scar the surface. Scarring is necessary for bonding and if omitted, the second coat will hold intermittently and peel in strips.

The third coat is applied in a manner identical to the second. Additional coats are counterproductive.

Wax or any other floor "finish" should not be used. They are parasitic products that perpetuate their use by requiring regular and ongoing renewal. Maintenance consists of damp or dry dust-mopping. Polyurethane resists staining by household materials. Spills that are allowed to dry usually come away with soap and water or by wiping lightly with a rag dampened in turpentine.

Although polyurethane develops a hard surface, it will scratch if something sharp is dragged over it.

Scratches are masked by rubbing lemon oil into them.

A three-coat polyurethane floor can be expected to last for ten years with normal use, and probably a good deal longer.

Installing 1-×-8 Maple Plank Floor

Laying wooden floors becomes progressively more difficult as wider boards are used. One cannot hope to close gaps between boards 8 inches wide and irregularities that cause them are removed before installation by a simple technique called straightlining.

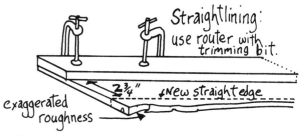

Fence clamped for straightlining with router

The illustration shows how straightlining is done with a router. I stretch a string along the side of the board and mark the narrowest place. I clamp a length of channel aluminum (or any very straight material) 2 3/4 inches in from the narrowest place and use it as a fence. I maintain the router against the fence throughout the length of the board and trim. Since the fence is straight and the router cutting parallel to it, the side of the plank is as straight as the fence. I straightline the other side of the board, then tongue and groove the sides. I cut the ends squarely and tongue and groove them. I prepare all the maple boards needed in the same manner.

I pop a chalk line 8 inches from either wall that lies at a right angle to the joists and will align the first course with the chalk line. I pop additional chalk lines that correspond to the centers of joists. I lay boards on the floor in the position they are to be installed and mark locations of joists. I bore holes 1/2 inch from the groove side at each joist location and facenail the planks with #8 finishing nails through the predrilled holes and into the joists. I machine-nail at joists along the tongue side.

In some installations, successive courses are simply machine-nailed along the tongue and prove sufficient. In other, side-nailing alone resulted in convex warping at the center of the planks and occasional curling along the sides. Warpage is a function of temperature and humidity extremes and difficult to anticipate in less severe situations. The prudent thing is to secure the planks along the central areas.

The simplest method is to nail the planks to every other joist, placing the nails 2 1/2 inches or so in from each side. The nails should be driven at a toenail angle to keep them from working loose. Nailheads are countersunk and the hole filled with maple-colored putty. The filled holes are not very conspicuous but certainly not invisible.

An alternative is to facenail the planks with aluminum horseshoe nails that emphasize rather than mask their presence.

The best procedure is called pegging. (Wooden pegs are no longer used.) To peg a plank, I bore a 1/2-inch-diameter hole 1/4 inch or so deep at a joist location. (I recommend the use of a Greenlee bit for boring because it produces a sharp, clean, and exact hole.) I position the plank and continue the hole with a 1/8-inch bit to a depth of 2 1/2 inches or so. I drive a #10 2 1/2-inch screw through the plank and into the joist. The head of the screw lies 1/4 inch or so below the surface of the plank. (Since maple, a hardwood, is being used, it's advisable to coat screws with parafin for easier installation.) Many screws will be needed and a Yankee screwdriver is recommended.

To fill the hole, I need a hand tool called a plug cutter. The plug cutter is a piece of hollow steel with a sharp circular tip a hair larger than 1/2 inch in diameter. The plug cutter is simply hammered into a scrap piece of maple and cuts a circular plug. I spread epoxy glue on the back and circumference of the plug, press it into the hole, and hammer it down. Part of the plug remains above the surface of the plank and is removed during sanding.

If I wish to minimize the presence of the plugs, I select grains that are similar to the adjacent grain of the plank. If I wish to emphasize the presence of the plugs, I choose mahogany or walnut scraps as stock for the plugs.

One plug centered on the plank over each joist is usually sufficient to prevent warpage and, combined with side-nailing, makes a secure installation. Two pegs spaced 2 1/2 inches in from each side at every joist is best for areas that have severe climatic changes.

The plank floor is finished with polyurethane as previously described.

White pine planks, because of their relative softness and susceptibility to marring, are not ordinarily used for flooring. However, if the addition is to be used as a bedroom and traffic is minimal, white pine (or fir) is a viable alternative when a hardwood cannot be obtained at a reasonable cost. All options previously described for oak and maple are applicable to white pine or fir. Sanding and finishing are identical.

Installing a Slate Floor

The techniques for quarrying and shaping slate and preparing mortar to the proper consistency have already been detailed. All pieces should be laid out on the floor and the needed fitting and arranging completed before installation is begun. Each piece should be marked with chalk lines matched to adjacent pieces to facilitate placement during installation.

I pop level chalk lines along the walls at the desired height of the finished floor. Although I will lay most pieces of slate by eye, whenever I am in doubt about the level of the particular one, I stretch a string between opposite chalk lines and use it as a reference.

I prepare a batch of mortar. I wet the slate and dampen the slab in the corner farthest from the door, where I will begin. I deposit a bed of mortar 1 1/4 inches or so thick, lay the first piece into it, and tap it down to decrease the thickness of the bed to 3/4 inch or so. Using the chalk marks on the stone (and wall for this first piece), I shift the piece as needed to re-establish it in the identical position it occupied before installation. For this first piece only, I lay one end of a level at the chalk line on the wall and the other end on the highest point of the slate. I tap the slate down farther if needed so that its highest point is level with the chalk line. I tap as needed, judging by eye, to bring the piece as a whole into level. I remove excess mortar along the edges adjacent to pieces still to be laid. The excess mortar is removed so that no continuous contact is made between the first and successive stones. In laying other stones, the necessary shifting about will cause the first stone to shift out of position if the mortar is contiguous. In effect, each piece of slate is laid independently and the gap between it and adjacent pieces already installed filled with mortar *after* alignment has been completed.

After having leveled the first stone, I use it as a reference. After laying the second stone, I fill the gap between it and the first with mortar. I continue in the same manner throughout the installation.

Mortar deposited in gaps between stones is sliced with the side of the trowel several times in order to pack it and make sure that it is filling hollows. Packing also causes increased bonding strength throughout the mortar and better adhesion to slate surfaces and the slab.

After laying a patch and still within arm's length of the corner, I scrape off excess mortar around the joints with a 3-inch pointed trowel and wipe off mortar from the surface of the slate with a wet sponge. Several passes with the sponge and frequent rinsing in clean water are necessary to remove the mortar.

I proceed in the same fashion, completing patch by patch until the entire floor is laid.

The floor should not be walked on for at least a day and several weeks should be allowed before normal use. (The installation will continue to gain strength for a month or so.)

After a month has elapsed, excessively high or irregular areas are lowered or smoothed by chipping with a cold chisel.

Slate requires no finish, but if a wet look is desired motor oil (either new or used crankcase oil) can be rubbed into it to enhance the color and provide a sheen.

(Masonry yards carry metalic oxides that provide various colors to the mortar. They are powders and are mixed into the mortar at the time of preparation. Colors are permanent.)

Installing a Split-Stone Floor

The procedure for laying split stone is essentially the same as for slate. Each piece is laid individually and the gap between it and adjacent stones filled with either mortar or an additional stone if the gap is excessively wide. If more than a hundred pieces are needed, I would consider renting an impact chisel to do the splitting; if fewer, use either a pickaxe or cold chisel and 2-pound hammer. The stone to be split should be placed on soft earth to provide a cradle so that when blows are delivered the stone doesn't go flying off. It is also advisable to use goggles when splitting stone.

Each stone is laid on its own bed of mortar, and only after it is positioned are the gaps between it and adjacent stones filled with additional mortar.

Unlike slate, which has a relatively uniform color, split stone often contains many colors. The final appearance of the floor should be considered prior to installation. A minimal choice is either to a light or a dark floor. One should also consider emphasizing particular areas with yellow and orange or minimizing other areas through the use of earth tones. Given the almost unlimited availability of colors, a good floor requires some prior thought on how to use them.

Once the stone has been split, no further shaping work is required. One should allow a week or so of work to prepare and lay a split-stone floor.

Installing a Used-Brick Floor

At first glance bricklaying appears to be a simple act but one learns quickly that appearances are deceptive and without sound techniques, a satisfactory job is highly unlikely. Approximately 1500 bricks are required (excluding the bathroom) and since each is laid individually, mistakes are repeated 1500 times and at best the floor will take an inordinately long time to lay.

A common arrangement of bricks in a floor is end to end in a straight line. Although I will detail this installation, the same techniques are applicable to other designs.

I prepare used brick for reuse by chipping off old mortar with a brick hammer. Prior soaking of bricks in water is only of minor help and the double handling involved makes the practice inefficient. Except for the side that will be seen, the face, a meticulous job is unnecessary and bits of mortar that adhere can be disregarded.

The most essential part of successful bricklaying is proper consistency of the mortar. If too thin, the brick being laid drops of its own weight below the desired height. If too thick, the brick is either difficult or impossible to tap down, and if excessive force is used the brick will crack, displace other bricks, or both. The optimum consistency is that of toothpaste and is confirmed when the brick being laid requires merely a *light* tap to lower it to the desired height.

If the consistency is that of toothpaste but more force than a light tap is needed to lower the brick into the mortar, too much sand is present in the mix. Proportionate amounts of cream, cement, and water are added and the mortar remixed to toothpaste consistency.

With the proper consistency, if the brick sinks below the desired height of its own weight, too much cement and cream is present. Proportionate amounts of sand and water are added and remixed.

On hot and dry days mortar consistency becomes too stiff within fifteen or twenty minutes. Additional water should be sprinkled on and the mortar remixed to the proper consistency. On cold and wet days, simple remixing every twenty minutes or so is all that is needed.

Although bricks vary in size, for the sake of simplicity I will use average dimensions; 8 inches long, 4 inches wide, and $2\frac{1}{4}$ inches high. All bricks are soaked in water for several minutes before use or until displaced air bubbles disappear. Soaking a brick prevents it from withdrawing water prematurely from the mortar and thereby destroying its structural and adhesive strength. For the same reason, the slab is dampened with a water atomizer before mortar is laid on it.

Unlike concrete blocks that employ mortar only around their perimeters, bricks require a full bed—mortar dispersed throughout the bottom of the brick. A mortar bed on a slab should have a minimum thickness of $3/4$ inch and preferably thicker if heavier-than-normal use is anticipated (rolling a piano over it, for example).

Each brick will be laid to a straight and level string placed at the height of the finished floor. Each brick is laid separately from others and only after it is correctly positioned are joints with adjacent bricks filled. The optimum thickness of mortar placed under a brick is an amount that leaves the brick $1/2$ to $3/4$ inch above the string when initially laid on the mortar. The mortar should also occupy an area under the brick that is $1/2$ inch smaller on all sides so that when the brick is tapped down it will spread and fill the $1/2$-inch perimeter and cover the bottom of the brick completely. If the final thickness of the bed is $3/4$ inch, the optimum amount of mortar to lay for a brick is about the size of a closed fist.

I use a 10-inch pointed trowel to transfer mortar from the mortar board to the floor. I deposit it on the slab by stopping my stroke abruptly before the trowel hits the floor, an action that causes the mortar to slide off. (If mortar clings to the trowel, too much cement and cream is present.) I flatten the lump of mortar with the trowel. (If one is inexperienced laying brick, the mortar should also be scored with the side of the trowel in several places to increase its plasticity.) I lay a brick in the corner $3/8$ inch in from each intersecting wall. I tap down the brick with a brick hammer until its bed is $3/4$ inch. Using a small level, I tap as needed to level the long side and then the wide side. In the same manner, I lay a brick in the opposite corner. I tack nails to the walls behind the bricks and stretch a nylon string between them. By stacking an additional brick or two on those laid, I bring the string down to the height of the brick and shift it as needed so that it lies along the sides of each brick.

I now deposit enough mortar on the slab for five or six bricks and lay them to the string. I omit mortaring the ends. After the bricks are laid, I return to the first, fill the end joint with mortar and the joint at the wall, and fill the remaining joints between the other bricks and wall. I continue the first course in the same manner until I am less than the length of a brick from the brick in the opposite corner. I measure the gap, deduct $3/4$ inch for a mortar joint at each end and cut a brick to length.

To cut a brick, I place a brick chisel along the desired line and whack it. One blow is usually sufficient. (With practice, cutting can be done with the brick hammer by simply striking the sharp end along the desired line.) I lay the cut brick in the gap and fill the joints with additional mortar.

During the laying of bricks, one should avoid striking the string. The brick is therefore held between the inner tips of the thumb and forefinger (or middle finger also if needed) with the finger ends in as horizontal a position as possible. As the brick is swung toward the floor, it is turned to a horizontal position by eye and laid lightly on top of the mortar about $\frac{1}{4}$ inch away from the string.

One should immediately note which end of the brick is higher by comparing it with the string. As the high end is being tapped down (tapping should not be done at the very end since it causes the other end to rise but 2 inches or so from the end) I note whether the side nearest the string is higher or lower than the opposite side and tap accordingly 1 inch in from the edge. Tapping is done at a slight diagonal in order to shift both planes simultaneously into a level attitude.

After leveling the brick along its length and width, I tap the brick gently toward the string until it is the closest I can get without actually touching the string. I now tap the brick toward the previously laid brick until the gap between them is $\frac{3}{8}$ inch.

The string doesn't serve as a reference for leveling the width of the brick and before one can do it by eye, a small level should be used.

The $\frac{3}{8}$-inch gap between bricks is determined by eye once the facility is achieved (the eye can learn to recognize $\frac{3}{8}$ inch in a surprisingly short time) and any scrap of $\frac{3}{8}$-inch-thick material can be used at the start as a reference.

If a short length of brick is needed to complete a course, $2\frac{1}{2}$ inches or less, striking with a brick chisel will not break the brick along the desired line. This must be done by starting with an already broken brick and reducing the length to size by chipping with a brick hammer along the edges until the desired length is achieved. Blows are delivered at an angle and away from the brick.

Bricks should be brought into the addition in a wheelbarrow and the wheelbarrow then filled with water to soak the bricks. *Wetted* bricks are stacked 3 feet behind the work area and at three intermittent points along the wall to avoid needless walking back and forth. For the same reason, it is advisable to have three mortar boards, each held up by concrete blocks on end. In the raised position, they eliminate a good deal of stooping for mortar.

After I have completed the first course, I shift the string 4 $\frac{3}{8}$ inches away to serve as a reference for the second course, allowing a $\frac{3}{8}$-inch joint between courses. By popping level chalk lines along the walls that lie at right angles to the courses and at finished floor height, I maintain the level of the floor. I begin the course with a half brick so that the

joint of each succeeding brick will lie halfway along the brick of the first course. I install the second course in the same manner as the first.

I shift the string for each successive course, using the chalk lines as a finished floor-height reference throughout.

When I am within several feet of finishing, I measure the remaining width and make joints slightly wider or narrower as needed to complete the floor with bricks of full widths.

The finished floor can be walked on after twenty-four hours, but several weeks should be allowed before normal use.

Installing a Mosaic-Tile Bathroom Floor in a Masonry Bed

Bathroom floors are subjected to a good deal of water and a masonry bed is optimum. Floors that employ mastic on underlayment are liable to severe deterioration due to seepage. Loosened tiles are common and rotting of underlayment or structural members also occurs. In addition, ceramic-tile floors installed with underlayment and mastic are more expensive than trouble-free masonry ones and involve more labor.

The simplest way to install a ceramic-tile floor is to steel-trowel the slab to a smooth finish while it is still plastic and later lay the tile with mastic directly on the slab. However, this places the height of the bathroom floor well below that of the other floors. Only a small amount of additional work is needed to bring the height of the bathroom floor into the same plane as the other floors and also to provide an optimum masonry bed.

To make the masonry bed, I prepare a mixture of 1 part cream, 10 parts cement, and 30 parts sand. The amount required ($1\frac{1}{2}$ inches thickness is a minimum) depends on how high the bathroom floor is to be and is calculated by multiplying the length, width, and depth of the bed to obtain the volume in cubic feet. (A bag of cement is one cubic foot.) I dry mix the material in a wheelbarrow with a hoe.

I move all the dry mixture to the back of the wheelbarrow, add water to the front, and begin to mix. I want a consistency that is much thicker than mortar. The preparation is called a dry mix, a misleading term since all the material must be wetted. The heavier consistency resists deformation much more readily than a looser one and makes laying tile easier. The optimum consistency utilizes the minimum amount of water needed to entirely wet the mix and still be barely able to keep its surface together when a trowel is passed over it. When a trowel is depressed forcibly into the mix, no water should exude from it.

After dampening the concrete, I dump half the batch onto the floor near the corner farthest from the door. I spread the mix with a wooden trowel and use the previously installed baseboard tiles as a height and level reference. I want the mix to lie flat and be level with the bottom of the baseboard tiles. I prepare a patch of bed no larger than arm's length from the corner.

I stroke the surface of the bed on a slight diagonal with a 1 × 3 held on edge to obtain a flat and level surface.

I apply a thin film of masonry adhesive called neet, a cementatious product that is the masonry equivalent of mastic. An alternative is a product called Dryset that also acts as an adhesive. (Average amounts needed are printed on the container.) I spread the neet over the surface in a $1/16$-inch-or-so film. I place a sheet of mosaic tile in the corner so that its sides are parallel to the intersecting walls and a gap of $1/16$ inch or so is left at the baseboard tiles.

I avoid shifting individual tiles. If necessary, I move an entire row by aligning them with the side of the rectangular trowel. I cover the patch with additional sheets, leaving a $1/16$-inch gap between sheets.

If it becomes necessary to cut tiles, I need only a nipper, a hand tool similar to pliers. The ends of the jaws are $3/4$ inch wide and ground to a sharp edge. To cut a tile, the edges of the nipper are placed at the desired line and the handles squeezed together. Small extensions on the handles prevent the jaws from closing completely and ruining the sharp edges.

When I have covered the patch with tile, I lay a piece of 2 × 4 on the tile and tap them down into the mix. I need to depress the tiles $1/16$ inch or so and only light tapping is necessary. I wipe off excess mix squeezed up between joints with a wet sponge.

I continue to install the floor by completing patches.

I cut away individual tiles or rows as needed by slitting the backing with a sheetrock knife.

A close fit is unnecessary around the water-closet flange and I lay only full tiles around it.

I butt the last tiles to the addition floor and cover the joint between them with either a chrome or marble saddle. The chrome saddle has predrilled holes for screws and is attached to the addition floor. (It is also tapered and will hide small variations in height between the two floors.)

The marble saddle may be installed over the tile or in the same plane by laying it into the mix at finished floor height.

The mix squeezed up through gaps between tiles takes the place of grout and no further treatment is necessary at the joints.

The floor can be walked on after a day and is ready for normal use within four or five days.

FINISHING THE ELECTRICAL WORK AND PLUMBING

7

Finishing the Electrical Work

During roughing in, a double gem box was installed beside the bathroom doorway and it is here that I begin the finishing work.

The illustration shows an electrical device called a ground fault interrupter to be installed on the left side of the double box. It is a duplex receptacle equipped with a very sensitive circuit breaker and its purpose is to shut off electricity to the circuit if any dangerous situation arises. For example, if a baby places the ends of a hairpin in the outlet slots, the GFI breaker switch will automatically trip extremely quickly and the baby will feel only a slight tingle rather than a severe jolt. Power is restored by simply depressing the circuit-breaker switch located on the face of the device. A second switch marked with a T (for testing) is used to determine whether the device is operational. The GFI fills a legitimate safety need and in a few states is now mandatory for bathroom and outdoor circuits.

On the left side of the double box are two cables; one has come to the box from the main (where it is still unconnected) and has been marked by a piece of electrician's tape; the other runs to the next

closest outlet located in the room. I want to attach the GFI to the cable from the main in order to have all power to the rest of the circuit routed through it and thereby provide the safety feature to all the remaining outlets and lights. (By attaching the GFI to the cable from the main, all other ordinary outlets are protected and the GFI will trip its break-

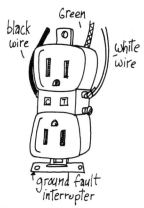

Ground fault interruptor

108

er if a dangerous situation arises in any of them.) The GFI has three wire leads extending from it; the insulation of one is green, a second white, and the third black. I strip ⅝ inch of insulation from the ends of all three wires.

I remove the tape on the cable from the main, place a stripping tool over it at the point where it enters the box, close the jaws of the tool, and pull it toward me. The tool slits the outer insulation, I peel it back and clip it off with wire cutters.

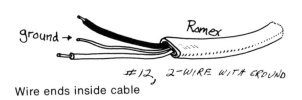

Wire ends inside cable

With the outer insulation removed, three wires inside the cable are exposed. One wire has white insulation, another is black, and the third is bare copper. I strip ⅝ inch of insulation from the ends of the white and black wires. I place the end of the white wire beside the white wire end of the GFI and join them by screwing a solderless connector (wire nut) over the two. (Older types of wire nuts are manufactured in various sizes that correspond to the thickness and number of wires to be joined. Newer types are self-adjusting to a variety of thicknesses and numbers of wires and should be used to avoid the hassle of selecting the proper wire nut. Older types have rigid bakelite housings, newer types are flexible plastic.)

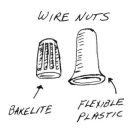

Bakelite and flexible plastic wire nuts

I place the stripped end of the black wire from the cable adjacent to the black wire end from the GFI and join them with a wire nut.

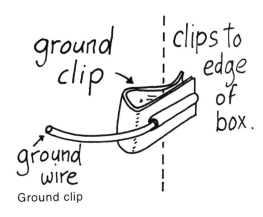

Ground clip

Pictured is a ground clip that is used to attach the grounding (bare) wire to the metal box. The end of the bare copper wire of the cable is inserted into the center hole of the ground clip and the clip pushed onto the edge of the box. Excess grounding wire is clipped off. Similarly, I attach the green wire end from the GFI to the metal box with a ground clip.

On each side of the GFI are pairs of screw terminals. On one side the terminals are brass-colored and on the other side they are silver-colored.

I strip the outer insulation of the cable that continues to the next nearest outlet and strip 1 inch of insulation from the end of the *black wire*. I form the end into a loop with needle-nosed pliers, loosen a *brass-colored terminal of the GFI,* install the loop under it in a clockwise direction, and tighten. (Since tightening is done clockwise, the loop is placed in a corresponding position to prevent it from opening as the terminal is tightened.)

Similarly, I strip 1 inch of insulation from the end of the *white* wire, form a loop, and attach it to the *silver-colored* terminal on the opposite side of the GFI.

I attach the bare wire to the metal box with a ground clip.

This completes the attachment of wires on the left side of the box.

On the right side of the double box is a cable that continues to the fixture box mounted above the basin, and I need to install a switch to control the light. I begin by stripping the outer insulation of the cable to expose the three wires inside.

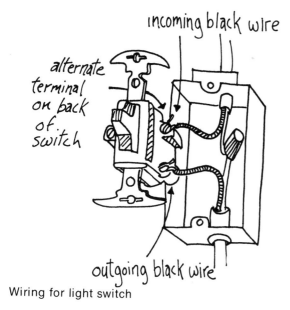

incoming black wire

alternate terminal on back of switch

outgoing black wire

Wiring for light switch

Pictured is an ordinary light switch that has two screw terminals along its side and two corresponding holes in the back that may also be used for attaching wires. I strip 1/2 inch of insulation from the end of the white wire and leave it for the moment. I strip 3/8 inch of insulation from the end of the black wire and insert the stripped end into the lower hole at the back of the switch. A clamp at the base of the hole secures the wire end. I attach the bare copper wire to the metal box with a ground clip.

I cut an 8-inch length of cable, strip off the outer insulation, and remove the white and black wires. I strip 1 inch of insulation from one end of the white wire and 5/8 inch from the other end. I attach the 1-inch-stripped end to the silver-colored unused terminal of the GFI and join the other end to the white-wire end of the cable with a wire nut. I strip 1 inch of insulation from one end of the black wire, and 5/8 inch from the other end. I attach the stripped 1-inch end to the brass-colored unused terminal of the GFI and insert the other end into the upper hole at the back of the switch. This completes the attachment of all wire ends in the double box.

I fold excess wire accordion-style, push the GFI against the box, and attach it with machine screws through the slotted holes at top and bottom and into the threaded holes of the box.(The slots permit adjusting the GFI to a centered position.) Similarly, I attach the switch to the box with two machine screws. (All necessary screws are provided with the purchase of all electrical items.)

I attach the cover plate over the GFI with a short machine screw through a center hole. The GFI has a threaded hole that is matched to the hole in the cover plate. I attach the cover plate of the switch with two machine screws that match threaded holes in the body of the switch. This completes the installation at the double box.

I strip the outer insulation of the single cable emerging from the fixture box and remove 5/8 inch of insulation from the ends of the white and black wires. I strip 5/8 inch of insulation off the ends of the white and black wires of the fixture. I place the stripped end of the white wire of the cable against the white-wire end of the fixture and join them with a wire nut. I place the black-wire stripped end of the cable beside the stripped end of the black wire of the fixture and join them with a wire nut. I attach the bare copper wire of the cable to the metal box with a ground clip.

I place the canopy of the fixture against the fixture box, align the predrilled holes of the fixture with those of the box, and attach the fixture to the box with two machine screws. This completes the installation of the fixture and the wiring for the bathroom.

The nearest outlet is located on the opposite side of the bathroom wall in the doorway area. It contains two cables, one coming in from the double box in the bathroom and another that continues to the next nearest outlet.

The back of a duplex receptacle is shown here. It has two pairs of screw terminals on each side; one pair is brass-colored, the other silver-colored. Each pair is located on opposite sides of the receptacle. Two rectangular holes in the back of the receptacle may also be used to connect wire ends. (A round hole beside each is provided to remove an attached wire. A nail is depressed into the round hole and spreads the clamps holding the wire ends.)

I strip the outer insulation from both cables. I strip 3/8 inch from the end of the *white* wire of the

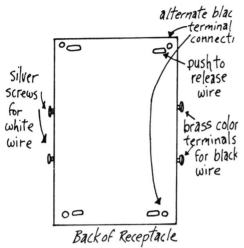

Back of duplex receptacle

hole at the back of the switch. I strip ³/₈ inch from the outgoing black wire end and attach it in the upper rectangular hole at the back of the switch. I strip ⁵/₈ inch of insulation from both white-wire ends, place them together, and join the ends with a wire nut. I attach both bare copper wires to the box with ground clips. I attach the switch to the box with two machine screws and install the cover plate.

I install the ceiling fixture in exactly the same way as described for the fixture above the basin.

This completes the wiring in the addition and only the final step of connecting the incoming cable in the main remains.

I go to the main and switch the main breaker to the *off* position. I remove four screws in the corners of the main's cover plate and remove the plate.

incoming cable and insert it into the rectangular hole of the receptacle on the *silver-colored* terminal side. I strip ³/₈ inch from the end of the incoming *black* wire and insert it into the rectangular hole on the *brass-colored* terminal side. I attach the bare wire to the box with a ground clip.

Similarly, I strip the ends of the white and black wires of the outgoing cable, insert the white wire into the remaining rectangular hole on the silver-colored side and the black wire into the rectangular hole on the brass-colored side. I attach the bare copper wire to the box with a ground clip.

At the top of the receptacle is a green hexagonal screw that is used for additional grounding. It continues the path of the third rounded prong at the plug end of a lead-in cord. I attach one end of a piece of bare copper wire to the hex screw and fasten the other end to the box with a ground clip.

I fold the wires accordion-style and push the outlet against the box. I attach the receptacle to the box with machine screws and install the cover plate.

In exactly the same manner, I proceed from receptacle to receptacle and install each in its box.

I arrive at the switch box beside the doorway to the house. There are two cables, one coming from the outlet nearest it and the other going out to the ceiling fixture box.

I strip the outer insulation from both cables. I strip ³/₈ inch of insulation from the end of the black incoming wire and attach it in the lower rectangular

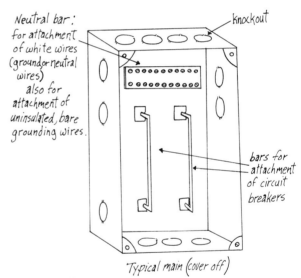

Typical main

Illustrated is a typical main. At first glance it appears terribly complex, but if a few minutes are taken to study the arrangement of wires, it will be seen that all white wires are connected to a horizontal bar at the top that has a great many silver-colored terminals. All the black wires (or red or any other color except white or green) are connected to circuit breakers mounted on two parallel vertical bars below the horizontal bar. The three incoming cables from the meter are thickest. The red and black wires are attached to terminals of the main breaker (the topmost and largest). The largest white wire is connected to the largest terminal of the horizontal (neutral) bar. An additional thick bare copper cable is connected to the neutral bar and continues either to a cold water main coming into the house or to a driven ground (a length of conductor driven into the ground).

With the main breaker switched off, only the incoming cables from the main still contain electricity but since their ends lie within the body of the breaker and are insulated elsewhere, there is no possibility of being shocked but a good practice is nevertheless to keep screwdrivers and other tools *away from the red and black wire ends entering the main breaker.*

I remove a knockout along the side of the main that permits closest entry of the cable. I slip the threaded half of a Romex connector over the end of the cable, insert the cable end through the knockout and pull till tight. I secure the threaded half of the connector to the cable at the knockout and attach it to the box with the locknut of the connector placed inside the main. I strip off all outer insulation of the cable that extends from the main.

A typical breaker is shown here. At the lower end is a hole and a set screw that is used to connect the *black* wire end.

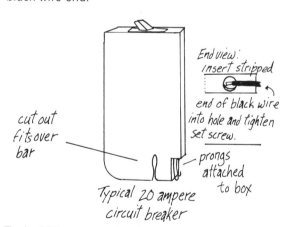

Typical 20-ampere circuit breaker, single-pole

I strip $1/2$ inch of insulation from the end of the black wire, insert it fully into the hole at the bottom of the breaker (there is only one hole), and tighten the set screw against the wire end to secure it to the breaker. I place the breaker directly below the lowest installed breaker, hook the two prongs at its lowest end on the vertical bar at the right, then press the cutout in the breaker body onto the vertical bar at the left. I fold excess black wire out of the way around the side of the main.

I strip 1 inch of insulation from the white-wire end and attach it to any unused terminal of the neutral bar (terminals are large silver-colored screws).

I attach the bare copper wire to any unused terminal of the neutral bar.

Along the front of the cover of the main is a series of rectangular slots that are partially cut and similar to knockouts. With a screwdriver and hammer I loosen the slot that corresponds to the position of the new breaker and remove it by twisting back and forth with pliers. I reinstall the cover with machine screws in each corner, switch on the main breaker and the newly installed one. This completes the entire electrical installation.

Finishing the Plumbing

During roughing in, a 3-inch DWV pipe for the toilet drain was installed 12 inches from the finished wall (or 14 inches if a lowboy or similar type was projected). The drain was cut off at a height that allowed for the attachment of a closet flange that would rest on the finished floor. The $1 1/2$-inch basin drain was centered in the projected center of the basin and brought through the wall at a height of 16 inches above the finished floor. The $1 1/2$-inch drain for the tub was completed during roughing in. Half-inch capped copper pipe was brought through the wall on each side of the basin drain to supply hot and cold water. The cold water supply from the basin was continued to the bowl area. Hot water supply from the basin was continued to the tub area and cold water supply was obtained by continuing the pipe from the bowl. The hot and cold water supply to the tub was connected to a special fitting 8 inches above the tub and centered on the tub drain. Pipe was continued to the shower from the special fitting to supply water and brought through the wall with a threaded male fitting. A short length of pipe was installed from the special fitting downward to the spigot location 2 inches above the top of the tub and brought through the wall with a threaded male fitting at the end. This is the situation that exists as the work of finishing the plumbing is continued.

I spread DWV solvent glue around the end of the 3-inch waste pipe and the interior of the closet flange. I slide the flange down over the pipe to the pipe's shoulder and the flange lies against the finished floor. I rotate the flange so that its slots along the circumference lie parallel to the wall. I insert the heads of bolts into the wide portions of the slots and slide them to portions that are narrower than the bolt heads. I place each bolt (head down) equidistant from the wall. (Bolts are provided with the fixture.)

I unfold the cardboard fixture boxes on the floor and lay the bowl upside down on it. I roll plumber's putty between my hands and shape it like a rope $1/4$ inch or so thick. I lay the putty around the perimeter of the bowl's base.

I place a 3-inch wax ring around the bowl outlet. (Wax rings are available at any plumbing supply house.)

I turn the bowl over and lower it so that both upright bolts in the flange come through predrilled holes in the base's sides. I press the bowl down with moderate pressure in order to seat the wax ring and also depress the putty. I place a washer around each of the bolts and secure the bowl to the flange with nuts until all movement has ceased and the bowl is snug. I am careful not to tighten the nuts excessively since the bowl is china and easily cracked.

I secure the tank to the bowl with rubber washers, bolts, and nuts provided with the fixture. Predrilled and matched holes are provided at the bottom of the tank and the rear of the bowl.

I shut the cold water valve in the addition main, place a pan under the nipple of the bowl supply, and cut the nipple an inch or so from the wall with a small pipe cutter. I allow the water to drain, place a piece of sheet asbestos against the wall behind the nipple, and solder a male fitting to the end.

I place an escutcheon over the pipe and against the finished wall.

A $1/2$-inch male fitting emerges from the bottom of the tank. I obtain a length of flexible chrome pipe for connection of the water supply. The flexible pipe is preassembled with a shut-off valve and nuts at each end. I tighten the nut at one end to the fitting from the tank and attach the nut at the opposite end to the fitting soldered to the nipple. The shut-off valve lies at the lower end of the flexible pipe. (Flexible pipe is available in various lengths.)

I attach the seat to the bowl with nuts and rubber washers and the installation of the toilet is complete.

I unscrew the cap over the shower nipple, place one turn of Teflon tape around the threads of the male fitting, place an escutcheon over the pipe, and screw on the shower head.

I remove the protective cardboard cylinders around the valves attached to the special fitting, place escutcheons over them, and tighten the three handles to the valves with single center screws. (Some handles have wedge-fitted plastic covers that have to be pried out to expose the center hole.)

I remove the cap from the nipple 2 inches above the tub, wrap the male fitting with Teflon tape for a single turn, and screw on the spigot. I wrap cardboard around the spigot to protect the finish while tightening with a Stilson wrench. The outlet of the spigot faces down. No escutcheon is necessary since the body of the spigot is flared to hide irregularities around the nipple. This completes the installation of the tub.

If a wall-hung basin is to be used, a cast-iron hanger bar is first installed. The normal height of the basin is 30 inches above the finished floor but can be lower or higher for individual convenience. I attach the hanger bar with #10 $2 1/2$-inch wood screws installed in predrilled holes in the hanger bar and into the wood backing previously nailed in the wall. The basin's prongs are then slid into the corresponding brackets in the bar.

Wall-hung basins have largely given way to the use of drop-in types and cabinets. Drop-in basins are manufactured in round, oval, square, and rectangular shapes. Some are self-rimming; their edges are finished and lie above the surface of the countertop. Others require a chrome metal part called a Houdee ring for installation. The ring lies on top of the counter and the basin is flush. The basin is held by special fasteners attached to the ring and basin.

Self-rimming basins are supplied with a paper template that is used to determine the precise location of the basin in the counter and have adequate instructions for use.

I will be using a rectangular basin that is not self-rimming and obtain a ring matched to the basin. I place the ring upside down on the counter and shift it so that it is centered over the drain. I have the option of positioning it in respect to the wall provided I leave a minimum of 1 inch from the inner plane of the cabinet (not the counter). I need at least 1 inch to attach the special fasteners.

After placing the ring in the desired location, I square it to the wall and trace its outline on the counter. I remove the ring and draw a parallel outline $\frac{1}{4}$ inch smaller than the first. I intend to cut out the smaller outline and prop a couple of 2×4s under it to prevent the piece from falling before it is completely cut and damaging the counter. I drill a $\frac{1}{4}$-inch pilot hole along the interior of the smaller outline, insert the blade of a sabre saw, and cut out the smaller outline. I place the ring in the cutout to see if it fits snugly and doesn't bind anywhere. I trim, if necessary, until the ring fits into the opening smoothly.

I turn the faucet set upside down and lay a thin bead of plumber's putty around its perimeter. I insert the threaded faucet ends into the holes in the basin and tighten the faucet to the basin with locknuts from underneath the basin. (All nuts and fittings are supplied with the faucet set.)

I remove the caps from the water-supply nipples, cut the nipples 1 inch or so from the wall, and solder male fittings to their ends.

I lay a bead of plumber's putty on the counter around the cutout. I place the ring on top of the basin and lower both into the cutout.

The illustration shows the fastener (supplied with the ring) that is used to attach both ring and basin to the counter. With a helper holding the basin from above, I lay the hook end of the fastener over the reinforcing metal strip of the ring and tighten the screw against the underside of the basin. A portion of the fastener lies under the counter and as the screw is tightened sink and ring come together to secure the assembly. I space 8 fasteners around the sink.

Using the preassembled nuts at the ends of flexible pipe (valves are at lower ends), I attach the pipe to the cold water supply and the cold water faucet end and do the same for the hot water supply.

I place plumber's putty in the circular indentation around the basin drain hole, insert the upper half of the strainer and secure it to the basin from underneath with a rubber washer and locknut. I hand-tighten the nut since I will shortly be raising the strainer.

The tailpiece, a thin metal pipe with a flared end, is the next item to install. I place a plastic washer around the flared end and attach it to the threaded end of the strainer with a slip nut.

I insert the $1\frac{1}{4}$-inch outlet of the pictured S trap into the end of the tailpipe for a distance of an inch or so, then measure how high or low the other outlet is with respect to the drain pipe emerging from the wall. If the trap is higher, I must obtain a longer tailpipe. If it is lower, I measure the amount and saw off an equal amount from the end of the tailpipe with a hacksaw. (I ream out the resulting burrs inside the tailpiece.)

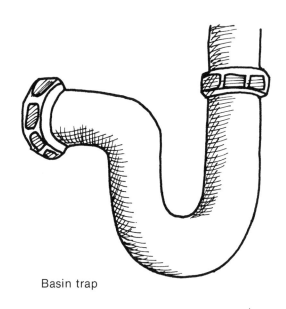

Ring fastener

Basin trap

I put the tailpiece back, insert the outlet of the trap, and mark the drain pipe at the end of the other outlet. I allow for penetration of the drain pipe into the shoulder of the trap and cut off the drain pipe.

I loosen the locknut holding the strainer and raise the assembly. I attach the 1½-inch outlet of the trap to the 1½-inch waste pipe emerging from the wall and turn the remaining outlet upward. I lower the tailpipe into the 1¼-inch outlet of the trap, tighten the locknut of the strainer with channel-lock pliers, then tighten the nut of the trap (and washer inside) to secure the tailpipe end inside it.

I attach the vertical bar that controls the up-and-down motion of the strainer-stopper to the horizontal bar underneath the basin with the provided nut or cotter pin. The vertical bar has a series of slotted holes; attachment is made through a hole that permits the stopper to open and close fully.

I remove excess putty around the ring and basin hole drain and the installation of the basin is complete.

I turn on the main water valves installed in the hot and cold water lines. Occasionally a leak is evidenced, almost always at a fitting. If the fitting is a nut and further tightening doesn't stop the leak, unscrew the nut, place pipe dope or Teflon tape over the threads, and retighten. Many of the fittings used have special threads that do not require pipe dope or tape, but from time to time they do not perform as advertised.

It is extremely rare for a leak to occur at a DWV fitting. Since all of the DWV installation was tested for leaks prior to closing the walls, if one does occur, it will be in an accessible area. Similarly, since all the water lines were tested prior to covering the walls, leaks at water-line fittings will also be in readily accessible areas.

If a leak occurs at a sweated joint, the water in the pipe must first be drained, the fitting heated and removed, pipe and fitting cleaned and resoldered.

The completion of the plumbing also completes the construction of the addition.

APPENDIX

Materials List for 20-by-20-foot Room and Bath Addition

Lumber

AMOUNT	MATERIAL	SIZE
92	2 × 4 hemlock fir	8′
52	2 × 4 hemlock fir	10′
24	2 × 4 hemlock fir	12′
9	2 × 4 hemlock fir	20′
3	2 × 8 hemlock fir	20′
6	2 × 10 hemlock fir	12′
74	T&G, V-joint 1 × 8 white pine	8′
300 square feet	V-joint 1 × 8 white pine	random lengths
360 square feet	1 × 8 maple	random lengths
8	1 × 3 white pine	8′
6	1 × 3 white pine	12′
12	1 × 3 white pine	10′
5	1 × 6 white pine	8′
14	5/4 × 4³/4 white pine	10′
3	1¹/2 × 6³/4 white pine	12′
6	5/4 × 2¹/4 white pine	14′
11	1¹/2 × 2¹/4 white pine	12′
11	¹/2 × 3¹/2 white pine	12′
3	¹/2 × 3¹/2 white pine	12′
21	¹/2″ plyscore	4′ × 8′
9	¹/2″ asphalt fiberboard	4′ × 8′
2	3/8″ exterior plywood	4′ × 8′

Multiply Your Living Space

Masonry

500 square feet	basalt stone	4'-6"
160 square feet	slate	random
40 square feet	split basalt	random
15 yards	bank run	
6 yards	ready-mix concrete	
3 yards	mortar sand	
27	cement	bags
14	mortar cream	bags
170 lineal feet	1/2" steel reinforcing rods	
15 lineal feet	ceramic baseboard tile	
140 square feet	ceramic tile	4 1/4" × 4 1/4"
1 gallon	waterproof wall mastic	
10 pounds	vinyl grout	
25 sheets	mosaic tile	1' × 1'
10 pounds	neet	

Insulation and roofing

500 square feet	fiberglass insulation	3 1/2"
400 square feet	fiberglass insulation	6"
500	random tab asphalt shingles	235-pound
8 rolls	15 pound felt	
6	1 3/4" × 1 3/4" aluminum edging	10'
25 lineal feet	aluminum flashing	14"
10 gallons	plastic roof tar	

Electrical

1 roll	#12, 2-wire Romex with ground	200'

1 20-ampere single-pole circuit breaker
9 gem boxes
2 fixture boxes
1 junction box
6 Romex connectors
12 wire nuts
7 duplex cover plates
7 duplex receptacles with ground
1 combination switch and receptacle cover plate
2 single-pole switches
1 blank cover plate for junction box
24 ground clips
1 ceiling fixture
1 wall fixture

Plumbing

3	3" PVC pipe	10'
3	1 1/2" PVC pipe	10'
1	closet flange	3"
1	closet sweep (ell)	3"
1	tee	3 1/2" × 3 1/2" × 3 1/2"
2 sanitary tees		3" × 3" × 1 1/2"
2	S traps	1 1/2" × 1 1/2"

8	PVC 45 ells	$1^{1}/_{2}$″ × $1^{1}/_{2}$″
4	PVC 45 ells	3″ × 3″
4	PVC sanitary tees	$1^{1}/_{2}$″ × $1^{1}/_{2}$″ × $1^{1}/_{2}$″
1	PVC cross fitting	3″ × 3″ × $1^{1}/_{2}$″ × $1^{1}/_{2}$″
1	cast-iron saddle fitting	3″
2	saddle tap tees	$^{1}/_{2}$″ × $^{1}/_{2}$″ × $^{1}/_{2}$″ ·
2	shut-off valves, sweat	$^{1}/_{2}$″
2	drain valves, sweat	$^{1}/_{2}$″
80 lineal feet	type L copper pipe	$^{1}/_{2}$″
5	sweat couplings	$^{1}/_{2}$″
15	sweat tees	$^{1}/_{2}$″
12	sweat ells	$^{1}/_{2}$″
5	sweat to male thread	$^{1}/_{2}$″
2	flexible pipe and valve	$^{1}/_{2}$″
1	basin, faucet set, and fittings	
1	bowl and tank and fittings	
1	cast-iron tub, faucet, shower, overflow and drain assembly	
1	chrome tub mold set	
1 roll	acid-core solder, 50:50 tin and lead	
1 can	flux	
1 pint	PVC solvent cement	
1	test cap	3″
2	test cap	$1^{1}/_{2}$″
1 sheet	fine emery cloth	
5	sweat caps	$^{1}/_{2}$″
1	recessed soap dish	
1	recessed soap dish with grab bar	
1	recessed toilet paper holder	
1 pound	plumber's putty	

Hardware
50 pounds #7 common galvanized nails
25 pounds #8 common galvanized nails
25 pounds #10 common galvanized nails
25 pounds #16 common galvanized nails
15 pounds #6 finishing galvanized nails
10 pounds $1^{1}/_{2}$″ wide-head roofing galvanized nails
108 #8 × 3″ lag screws
6 crank hardware sets
230 lineal feet $^{1}/_{4}$″ × $^{1}/_{8}$″ stainless U channel
230 swing screws
230 lineal feet aluminum screen stile stock
35 square feet fiberglass screening
230 lineal feet plastic spline
230 lineal feet T-shaped plastic weatherstripping
60 pieces 12″ × 40″ single-strength glass (63 pieces)
5 tubes silicone caulking
1 bedroom lockset
1 bathroom lockset
4 pairs 3″ × 3″ hinges
15 J bolts, $^{1}/_{2}$″ × 10″ with washers and nuts
160 gang-nail metal strips for trusses
2 pounds #8 aluminum finishing nails

Miscellaneous
1 panel door, 30″ × 80″
1 panel door, 28″ × 80″
2 sets doorstop, ³/₈″ × 1³/₈″
1 chrome saddle, 4″ × 28″

Essential tools (minimum)
20-oz. hammer
slot screwdriver, Phillip's-head screwdriver
pliers
crescent wrench
6¹/₂″ power saw, combination blade, masonry blade
2 50′ tape measures
folding rule with extension
8-point handsaw
³/₈″, ³/₄″, 1¹/₄″ wood chisels
2″, 4″ brick cold chisels
wheelbarrow
protractor
4′ level
ball of nylon mason's string
16″ rectangular trowel
10″ pointed trowel
18″ wood float
3″ spackling knife
sheetrock knife
propane torch
tubing cutter
hacksaw
¹/₄″ drill, ³/₄″, ¹/₈″ bits
framing square
T square
brace and expansion bit
metal-cutting shears
chalk line
stapler, ¹/₂″ staples (2 boxes)
sabre saw
wire cutters
wire strippers

Desirable tools
12″ radial-arm saw
Yankee screwdriver and bits
¹/₂″ 575-rpm drill, ³/₄″ × 16″ twist bit,
³/₄″ Greenlee spur bit
reciprocating saw
builder's level
2¹/₂-horsepower router, ³/₈″ rabbeting
bit, ¹/₈″ × ³/₄″ splining bit, ¹/₂″ trimming
bit, all carbide-tipped

8¹/₄″ Skil saw, heavy-duty
socket set with ¹/₂″ drive
2-pound hammer
channel-lock pliers
flat bar
cast aluminum 16″ and 48″ levels
cat's paw
chain vise

INDEX

[Page references in boldface refer to illustrations.]

Index

Index